THE EDGE
OF BROKEN

THE EDGE
OF BROKEN

FROM LOSING EVERYTHING TO BUILDING A BUSINESS EMPIRE.
A TRUE STORY.

LINDA WARD

ISBN: 978-1-7325674-0-5 (Paperback)

Published in Nashville, Tennessee by Duchess Books LLC. Duchess Book titles may be purchased in bulk for educational, business, fundraising, or sales promotional use. For information, please email hello@sincerelylinda.com

First print edition: 2018

Duchess Books LLC

www.SincerelyLinda.com

To my wonderful husband and two beautiful daughters, who helped me realize that there is so much to live for. You've molded me into the woman I am today.

CONTENTS

INTRO - DROWNING

The wind whipped thick strands of jet black hair into my face. I tried capturing as many clumps of unruly hair that my small hands could hold and tucked them as best as I could behind my ear. I felt the warmth of the blazing ocean sun on my back and glanced upwards at the vivid blue sky, squinting to see better through the bright summer day. Closing my eyes, I took in the sound of my family laughing and chattering, found solace in the cawing of the seagulls overhead, and felt sprinkles on my legs as the waves gently lapped against the side of our boat.

I looked down to my feet, only inches away from the water's edge. Sneaking a quick glance over at my brother, I smiled, determined to stretch my feet far enough to touch the cool water before he did. *There's no way I'm letting him win*, I thought. My 3-year-old brother Anthony was only a year younger than I was, and even at an early age, we were incredibly competitive as siblings. Being the eldest, I was a hard fight to the finish line in everything we did. I wasn't the type of girl who'd be outdone by a boy, let alone my own younger brother. I had no intentions of accepting defeat now, either.

We sat towards the back side of the boat, precariously on the slippery edge, instead of safely tucked into our seats. I grasped the edge of the boat as firmly as I could and stretched my feet further towards the water. I felt the tip of a wave weave through my toes and giggled, knowing I was so close to winning. In my adrenaline rush, I lunged my feet towards the chilly water, wanting to relish in the pride of beating him. I'm sure, from the outside looking in, the following events happened incredibly quickly. For me, the world slowed down, almost as if it was on the edge of stopping altogether. My excitement got the best of me. In my attempt to fully submerge my leg in the water, my hand lost its grip on the wet surface, and I fell off the boat.

I didn't have a vest on and had no clue how to swim. I felt the ocean slowly begin to pull me down into some 40 feet of water. I'll never forget the silence that followed when my head went under. The world as I'd known it disappeared, replaced with a distant hum and a vast blue sea. I could no longer smell the salt in the air, hear the voices of my parents talking with their friends at the front of the boat, or feel the heat of the sun. Everything disappeared. Now under the waves, I felt the coolness of the water against my sunburned skin. With my arms outstretched, I slowly sank further towards the bottom.

Surprisingly, I didn't feel fear. Not in that moment. The world had abrupted into chaos around me, but there, alone in the quiet, I felt an odd sense of peace. My thick black hair swam around my face, and through the strands that covered my eyes, I captured glimpses of fish swimming around my feet. I felt encompassed in energy greater than my own. An energy I felt entwined with. My sinking body was drowning, but instead of being lost in a sense of fear, I was mesmerized by the sensation that I was in another world. I gently turned to look in a new direction and saw the light of the sun flooding through the surface of the water. I stared into the yellow orb in a trance, captivated by how ethereal it seemed.

If anyone asked me what I thought death would be like, I would compare it to that moment. A freeing sense of weightlessness, absolute silence except for the quiet hum in the distance, and an ethereal orb of light that draws you nearer and nearer to it. I spent a majority of my childhood thinking that orb of light was an angel. It was only the way the light from the sun played in the water, but that moment still made me feel like I was in a different realm.

A slight tug on my arm pulled me out of my trance. I glanced up and felt my whole-body lunge upwards as my father grabbed my arm and pulled me into his chest. In a matter of seconds, my head broke the surface of the ocean and I was sputtering out water, trying to breathe in the thick salty air. My dad brushed my hair out of my face, "Are you okay?" he asked, worried. I shook my head yes and broke into tears. The realization of what occurred finally hit and I began to shake in a panic. My father huffed a laugh of relief, assured me I was safe and swam me back towards our boat. My mother's face, mixed with tension and relief, smiled back at us. The smile didn't reach her eyes.

That was nearly 21 years ago. There have always been bits and pieces to my past that my mind has completely blacked out. No matter how hard I try to go back to certain things in my childhood, I get lost in a dark void that remains empty. To protect me, I've heard. But I'll never forget that day. I'll always remember the sensation of the water, the quiet hum in the distance, and the sun and how it glowed in a beautiful orb under the sea. I hold onto that memory more vividly than trying to remember what I had for breakfast yesterday. It wasn't only till recently I figured out why. That moment in my life would be synonymous with the way the rest of it would pan out.

In that moment, that 4-year-old little girl was drowning. *I* was drowning. Even with death being only a minute or so of breath away, the world didn't seem chaotic - not from my point of view, anyway. Instead, there was an eerie and quiet stillness. I found peace in an ethereal sensation, almost out-of-body, but I was still gazing at the world through my own cloudy eyes. I lived most of my childhood in this state of being. Fully withdrawn into a beautiful new world my mind created, while the rest of the real world remained destructive. It felt like every day I was holding my breath, afraid to open my mouth to scream for help, in fear that I'd die from my last breath. I was dying inside for years without knowing it was happening. Strangers on the outside looking in wouldn't have noticed, but no one saw the things I saw. I was alone, the world was quiet, and my mind took me to beautiful places where my imagination blossomed with life – while my physical body was being tormented.

This is my story. It's a story of a little girl who lost everything in her life. In these upcoming chapters, I'm going to share with you that story, through my own eyes and emotions. Finally letting the world see the truth in a way I've never let anyone else in to see, not even the people I held closest to my heart. It's going to start off dark because most of my childhood was lived in a dark place. Despite the brokenness, the abuse, the homelessness, the depression and anxiety you'll read on about – this book will lead in another direction. This story isn't just about a little girl who lost everything, but also that of a woman who built her empire from that oblivion. It's not just about drowning through my childhood, it's about finding my breath and healing again. It's not just about the moments I pressed a cold blade against my wrist, my hand shaking as I cried in heavy sobs, but about the moments I put the knife down and wiped my tears away. This book is meant to inspire you, to encourage you, to motivate you, and to guide you. It's to share with you the story of a little girl the world determined would become another statistic; but instead, how she went on to conquer it. I'm sharing with you a story that I've held back from even talking to myself about for a long time, because it was just too hard to think about. But my past was a wound, and that wound would always remain infected and affect the way I lived the rest of my life. That is, until I decided to finally address it, cleanse it, and heal from it. This book is more than just about encouraging others, but also the final stitches on a past that I'm now ready to forget about and move on from. A past that I'm truly ready to heal from.

If there is anything you take away from my story, it's that we're all capable of surviving. Even more than that, we're entirely capable of thriving. I've spent over 20 years of my life surviving and I wanted it to be much more than that. I was ready to thrive, succeed, really live, and finally breathe. The only way to achieve that was to build a world around me that made that a possibility. I refused to be minimized by all the people that tried embedding in me that I'd amount to nothing. Their promise that I was a failure encouraged me to become something powerful. I made a commitment to myself that one day I'd stop falling asleep in tears and pain, so I had to focus on building a life that allowed me to fall asleep happy. This story of mine is also about a little girl that lived homeless in a tent, who then went on to buy a half-million dollar home in cash by the age of 25. Only to realize that money wasn't the solution to happiness - it just bought convenience.

I wrote this book for a specific group of people. It's for those who feel like they're on the verge of losing every bit of strength they've ever had. It's for those who feel worthless, angry, and broken. It's for those suffering through hard times, whether it's past or present, and desperately wanting to know that there *is* a way out. If you want a way out of emotional trauma and financial burdens, then I wrote this book to connect with you. No matter what form of pain you have, I want to encourage you to keep pushing – because, as evidenced in my own story, the will to fight on can open an endless supply of opportunities.

I hope my journey inspires you to become the best you can be. I hope it motivates you to tune out the white noise in a world that constantly tells you that you can't amount to anything, including the white noise in your own head. I want my story to give you the courage to go out there and build your own empire, in whatever shape and size you envision that to be. Outside of searching for your own way to become successful and wealthy, I hope this book inspires you to find happiness. That elusive happiness, that both the rich and poor are always chasing. If it could be bottled and sold, the owner of the answer to happiness would own the world. I haven't found the key to the door of absolute bliss, but I've found the right direction, and I hope you take this narrow road with me to unlocking it.

1.

THROUGH THE EYES OF A CHILD

I grew up in a small town in Turkey called Adana. My father at that time was in the American Airforce and had been stationed there by the age of 19. That was where he'd meet my mother and the two of them would throw themselves into an unexpected marriage after a night that would have left her shunned from her family, otherwise. Their relationship started off with infatuation and excitement, but their love was never meant for any storybook romance. That is, if you could even bother to call what they had love at all.

My mother, accompanied by my two younger brothers and I, spent most of her time at her parent's house while my father was at work. Despite my father's position in the military, we lived a poor life. As children, we didn't know exactly how poor we were until the future brought us to the United States and made our conditions in Turkey look third-world. Home to us was a small little house that didn't even so much as have a bathroom in it. Instead, we had an outhouse in the front of my grandparent's home that was a small little wooden building. It had a small little hole in the middle of the floor that we'd crouch over to handle business. We didn't have any toilet paper on hand, either. Instead, in the corner of the small space, sat a jug of water that was meant for cleaning up. We'd pour the water into our cupped hands and cleaned ourselves with it, front and back. The blistering heat did nothing to assist the foul odor that emanated from the pit the waste collected in. I'd smack the buzzing flies out of my face and sped through the process. I could never get out of there fast enough; the stench was unbearable.

We lived where our food lived. With chickens and goats all throughout the yard and at the back of the house. Aside from the fish we bought from a cart, pushed by a local fisherman, dinner was generally what you had on hand. That also included an assortment of fresh vegetables and fruits picked up at the local outdoor market. The inside of the home was in shambles, what you'd expect to see in a house that looked like it was staged with things even Goodwill couldn't sell. Not having a real bathroom also meant you didn't have a shower or tub to bathe in. Instead, we had a small stone room off the side of our kitchen. In the middle of the room sat a wooden stool and we'd occasionally be washed using a pot of lukewarm water my grandmother would heat over her stove.

Breakfast and lunch were always an informal event, with a menu that consisted of warm milk sweetened with sugar, a salted tomato sandwich, or some cooked spinach. Dinners generally became a little more extravagant. We'd invite the neighbors and nearby family members, who'd come together to use the fresh produce and livestock to cook meals from scratch. Although dinner was usually a lively affair, the most unforgettable supper was the one that left my 4-year-old heart broken. We had brought home a new lamb and I became absolutely infatuated with him. Looking past our biological differences, and his inability to communicate, I still considered him my first best friend. Unfortunately, he wasn't brought in to be kept as a pet but would be used for supper only a few days later. When that evening came, I was a heartbroken mess. In defiance, I refused to touch my dinner, in tears over the friend I had lost. My mother was furious. She told me tales of how horrifically I'd burn in hell if I didn't finish my supper. Terrified by her detailed stories of eternal damnation and torture, I ate my friend in tears, choking on heavy sobs.

Our playtime wasn't any more extravagant than our outhouse. Across the street, in an abandoned lot full of trash and mud, we let our creativity flow. We used empty cans and plastics to build mud pies and play house, catching whatever bugs we could find along the way. We thought ourselves lucky when we'd find a swarm of black and white striped Monarch caterpillars and would use an old shoebox to scoop them up and raise them. Running down dust-filled cobbled streets, most often barefoot, we found whatever form of entertainment available to us. Our play group consisted of a few kids that lived on our street, most of them cousins. On incredibly rare and special occasions, my grandparents would take me to the local market to grab a few cheap toys. They never brought my brothers along. I distinctly remember the day when we were walking down the street, my brothers chasing after us crying and begging to come along, and my grandmother lying that she was taking me to the doctor. I didn't know why she wasn't telling them the truth, but I was excited to be getting a real toy, so I didn't call her out on her lie. For unknown reasons to this day, my grandparents hated my brothers and always treated them ill. Odd, given that girls were low on the totem pole in our culture. We were considered property, even. Whatever toy she bought, I shared with my brothers afterwards, despite my grandmother's demand that I hide it from them.

Have you ever watched an American war film, based somewhere in the Middle East? It generally pans in over the city, with a melodic Muslim prayer sung over the speakers in the background. Across the ashen faces of young children, wearing ripped up clothing that wouldn't even be given away for free, who were kicking around trash as entertainment. That was our life. Dirty faces against a broken backdrop. Life was good, from our eyes, because it was the only life we'd known. If you were an outsider looking in, you would have seen the chaos of our life from the beginning. Those dirt streaked faces, smiling and laughing, had hair infested with lice. The one-year-old little boy, our brother Jesse, who was stumbling after us, had sat in a dirty diaper all day long and was now forming a nasty rash.

Our mother saw us more of a nuisance than her own children. She'd make a pathetic attempt to clean us up towards the end of the day, before she'd take us back to base housing to see our father. Those smiling young faces went to bed some nights with nothing more than stale bread to get them through the day. Some evenings, when we'd spend the night at my grandparents' home, my brothers would be sent to bed without a bite at all. So, I'd stash bread into my pockets to give to them in the middle of the night when the rest of the house was asleep. I don't remember my father in the picture most of my childhood, I know he was kept busy and away often because of the military, so memories of him in that time were far and in between. Most of the memories I could conjure up of him were the nights he and mom fought. Sometimes their fights were physical, but most often the shrill of my mother's angry voice would echo off the walls, only silenced momentarily when my father's deep bellowing words hollered back. I never understood what they fought about, but it was clear they couldn't stand each other.

My brothers and I did what we could to find joy in our lives, making each other laugh and finding humor in our own mischief. There wasn't much to keep us happy in our dark and abandoned corner of the world, so we leaned on one another to get us through. We took care of each other more than my mother ever took care of us. We'd find treasures in the world's trash and kept busy with our imaginations.

We buried away the nights we'd go to bed in tears because we were hungry. Buried away the days our mother would smack us so hard in the face, our heads would whiplash backwards. Buried away the days my brothers were sent out to polish shoes to make money to buy food. Buried away the threats that I'd be married off, once I reached my early teens, to bring financial security for the family. At an age when children should be taught to love each other and play nicely, my grandparents were busy pitting my brothers and I against each other in hopes of tearing our bond apart.

We had a small fortune of grace when my mother's sister started seeing first hand our mistreatment every time she visited. My aunt went to my father when she had the chance and let him know about the horrific neglect and treatment that went on when he was away at work. An already fragile marriage quickly began to fall apart at the seams. My father's disgust towards my mother and her side of the family grew. He couldn't understand why my grandparents would treat us, especially my brothers, so ill. Even more befuddled that our own mother would sit idly by and watch it all happen, lazy and neglectful in taking care of us herself.

My parent's separation became hostile. Mom directed her anger towards us and her abuse grew in severity. We were caught in the crossfire of a tumultuous relationship that was being bashed against the rocks. She'd furiously throw and break furniture and dishes and screamed constantly in a maniacal rage. Every frustration she had, she let out on us. We were an easier target than our 6-foot-8 father. When she wasn't burning my arm with a cigarette, she'd be holding a knife at my brother Anthony, reminding us of our uselessness and how much of a mistake we were in her life. We'd stand, huddled next to one another, crying and shaking in fear, not understanding what was going on, but feeling like we were at the root of all the problems. For every bit of hate she had for our father, she equally hated us.

The abuse became even more severe and consistent when dad started dating another Turkish woman through the duration of my parent's divorce. His relationship to his new girlfriend formed quickly and when my mother found out about "her replacement," she was consumed by her rage. Convinced that there was a daily conspiracy to ruin her life and turn everyone against her, even us kids, who she constantly reminded she hated.

It was a battle between my parents on who the children would stay with. Even though our mother couldn't stand the sight of us, she'd fight to keep us out of the hands of the man she despised and his new partner. The decision was laid on our shoulders when we were asked who we preferred over the other. Our father was being sent back to the U.S. and was taking his new girlfriend, while our mother would remain in Turkey. We were abused, hated, and broken, but had grown familiarity with our mother and her parents. For children so young, familiarity was comfortable – even despite the abuse. For that reason alone, we chose to stay with mom. My father was heartbroken by the news, but after a little persuasion and a heart-to-heart that evening, we ended up deciding to go to the U.S. with him. My mother didn't take the news lightly, but in the end, the ultimate decision came from the judge when she told him she wanted nothing to do with us. From there on out, we'd be in the fulltime care of our father.

• • •

Bags packed and the only life we'd ever known left behind, we went off to start a new life in the states. Barely speaking a word of English, fluent in Turkish, we set off to start a new chapter in a brand-new world. Leaving behind forever a mother who denied her three children a willingness to love them the way a real mother should. Being ripped away from a mother is hard enough on children, to be ripped away from a mother who didn't seem to even want them, well – it doesn't matter how old you are, that's something you'll carry with you for the rest of your life.

Starting off in a new world meant starting off on a new slate, and that meant we had a lot of cleaning up to do. My brothers and I had hair filled with hundreds of lice and lice eggs. The best way to get rid of lice was to get rid of the hair they infested. My brothers were buzzed to their scalps and my thick long locks were chopped nearly as short as theirs. The new style did nothing to compliment my features. By the age of 6, I'd be calling Texas my new home for the next few years. My father's girlfriend was now his fiancé and we were already conditioned to begin calling her mom. My brothers and I did our best to settle into this change of scenery.

It wasn't long before the tension began to build at home. Stress became a common theme for my father and his new bride-to-be. She was now pregnant with her first child, and this new life in the U.S., after spending all of it in Turkey, was a massive change for her as well. We did our best settling in, but soon we'd come to realize that we'd escaped our mother's explosive anger to begin a life getting to know the one our father had.

After a short stay in base housing, we soon moved into a dark blue double wide trailer. It looked like it came out of a southern romance. The blue was a deep indigo and was complimented with stark white shutters. In the backyard was a small field that bloomed with plump orange pumpkins. The sky always seemed a bright blue and it looked like the beginning chapters to a life full of happiness. A fresh start that promised adventure, laughter, and love. Unfortunately, an innocent child's world is always full of optimism and sometimes life just doesn't live up to it.

By the age of 7, my health began to deteriorate. I felt weak and exhausted all day long and spent most of the days lying on the couch, feeling ill. Every time I went to the bathroom to relieve myself, there was always a strong decaying odor that followed. On a trip, visiting my father's parents in Indiana, the family became concerned by my discoloration and increasing exhaustion. My parents were convinced it was time to run me to the hospital when I began peeing blood. I was pale and looked like I was on the cusp of death by the time a doctor saw me. After a few tests, it was discovered that my left kidney was dying from an undetected birth defect. By that time, it was completely shutting down. There wasn't a thing left to do but to get the kidney out in an emergency surgery. The date for surgery was set and I spent a few days in the hospital getting prepared for the procedure. Christmas that year was spent in the hospital. The children in the hospital had a special visit from Santa, who gifted me a little doll to lift my spirits. My parents brought me a beautiful Christmas edition Barbie and I'll never forget the stunning hue of her cobalt gown.

When the day of the surgery came, I was wheeled into the procedure room, and remember as I was put to sleep. It seemed only minutes later that I found myself awake and being wheeled back to my room. I squinted up at the bright white lights on the ceiling, trying to see through the thick haze. The sound of my nurse's footsteps, as she pushed my bed towards my room, pattered on the floor and I heard hospital machines beeping in the near distance. My throat felt sore and I tried clearing it with a small cough that shook my small body and rumbled through my abdomen. I screamed in sheer agony as it rattled its way down to my belly, the fresh wounds burned intensely.

The surgery was now over, and the doctor said everything had gone wonderfully. After being looked over for a few more days, I finally got the chance to go home. I did my best to take it easy to allow my body the opportunity to heal, spending most of my time indoors and on the couch. One evening, shortly after finishing dinner, I went to the bathroom to wash my hands. I suddenly became overwhelmed with the urge to use the toilet. My belly began to cramp, and I let out a quiet moan, pressing my hand against my belly in hopes of stopping the pain. I pulled my pants down quickly and sat down on the toilet to relieve myself. The room began to spin, and I trembled in a cold sweat.

I was overcome by apprehension, a foreboding sense told me something was really wrong. Slowly, standing up on shaking legs, I stumbled towards the bathroom door. My hands shook on the knob as I struggled to pull it open, now barely able to see through a cloudy vision. Using all of my strength to walk along the wall, I stumbled into the hallway and screamed for my parents as I collapsed on the floor. Rushing over and seeing the state of my condition, my father frantically grabbed the phone and called 911. My step-mother rushed over and sat by my side, assuring me everything would be alright. The color had completely drained from my face and I could hear the worry in her voice. "Dad's calling the ambulance, they'll be here shortly, just hang in there," she consoled. The concern in her voice was telling.

Then, as if someone had switched the lights off, everything around me went dark. "I can't see anything," I said, as an overwhelming panic took control of my senses. "I haven't closed my eyes and I can't see anything. Why can't I see anything?" Turning my head in different directions, forcing my eyes to open, even though I already knew they were, I tried desperately to see through the blindness. My step-mother held me, trying to comfort me with promises that everything would be okay. With the faint sound of ambulance sirens off in the distance, the world disappeared as I lost consciousness.

The next day, I woke up to excruciating pain in my stomach and back. My nostrils burned from where they had pulled out the breathing tubes. Feeling a fiery scratch in my throat, I did my best this time to hold back coughing again. The doctor, who had completed my kidney removal surgery only a few days before, had unknowingly cut a vein. This lead to massive internal bleeding. I had made it into the hospital only minutes before dying. Desperately, doctors and nurses clamored around my body, attempting to draw blood, but struggling to find a vein that produced any. I came on the verge of losing my life that night, but by God's grace, I lived through a tremendous amount of blood loss. What were small incisions in the first surgery was now a grotesque scar from under my breasts down to my pelvis. When the day came to finally go back home, I knew it would be a long journey before I healed and found enough strength to get back into a normal routine of life and school.

• • •

With four children now in our growing family, we still lived close to the poverty line. Although our house was a little nicer, food on the table a little more consistent, and had access to a real bathroom, we were still incredibly poor. My step-mother gave birth to my first sister, Victoria. With a new baby and a low income, stressful was an understatement regarding the atmosphere in the house. The stress began to deteriorate our family. A rift quickly grew between my step-mother and I. The older I got, the further we grew apart, to the point we couldn't stand to be in each other's presence. My father's tall frame with big bones made him a nightmare when he was angry, and he seemed to be angry most of the time during those days. His stress somedays got the better of him, making him snappy and swift with punishments. We grew up with the burn of a belt on our backends as familiar of a feel as the sting on our cheeks from his handprints. My brothers and I lived in fear of our dad, convinced that our step-mother manipulated stories to get us in severe trouble for minor childish antics. Dreading getting backhanded in the face, we tiptoed around him, in an effort not to trigger his anger. He was a hard man with a hard hand who didn't hesitate to punish as he saw fit. Used to his sudden strikes, we'd throw our hands up to cover our faces anytime his hand moved quickly in our direction. His green eyes would shine in his anger, making him look menacing and snake-like. At school, I'd get questioned often by my teacher or the counselor to explain the more prominent bruises. I repeated the script my father demanded, telling them I was prone to taking a spill down the stairs.

Life for my brothers and I were hard. We had lost an unloving mother and our new mother seemed to resent us. We felt detached from our father because of his explosive anger, afraid to ever get too close and make a mistake. Our childhood was lonely. My brothers and I held onto each other, the only bond we could find in a world that made us feel like we belonged to no one. Our beautiful redheaded sister didn't live in the shadow of my father's belt or in the irritated and disappointed glances from her mother, which grew a gap in our upbringing. Regardless of the difference in treatment, I adored Victoria. She was the most precious little girl I had ever seen; her hair was full of curly ringlets and shined like a fiery sun. Although I'd never view her as a half-sister, but instead as my own flesh and blood, my bond with my brothers grew deeper as the negative attention seemed to always fall on us.

We had left behind a life in Turkey with one form of pain and punishment, only to have come to the states to be thrown into a new one. We knew fear and anger better than we knew love, and what love we were most familiar with, came through the bond of my siblings. Being the oldest, I felt incredibly protective of them. I felt hopeless watching my father let his anger out on my brothers, helpless to do anything to save them against a man who towered over us. This was our life. Forever on edge, fearing our father and step-mother's attention, longing for moments they'd show us any form of love.

The military didn't keep us in Texas for long. After a few years, we were heading out to a new home and life in Germany. I fell in love with Germany, instantly. The air felt so clean to breathe, the trees were a vivid green – a stark contrast to the endless browns in Texas. I was captivated by Germany's eccentric culture. We moved around from base housing to old homes in small towns that looked like they hadn't changed for hundreds of years. Although the tension at home hadn't changed much from our life in Texas, age and repetition made my brothers and I more resilient.

Life in Germany felt simple, yet magical. We made great friends and had fun adventures. Finally, we started to have a glimpse of what it was like to live carefree, as a child should. We enjoyed touring the country with school field trips and I was mesmerized by the cathedrals and old Roman architecture. There was more leniency to our life in comparison to the States. A better sense of security to let your children outside without supervision, and without fear that something would happen to them. We'd walk to school or make 20-minute treks to gas stations by ourselves to pick up cigarettes for our parents and get Kinder eggs with the left-over change. There wasn't any sense of threat outside of the only one we knew at home. Germany was hit quite often with blizzards, so we grew up with the cliché of getting to say we walked through mounds of snow to get to school. A dusting of snow in

Texas shut down everything, but here in Germany, schools remained open no matter how angry the winters would get.

Always the entrepreneur, even at a young age, I remember my hunger and drive to start working so I could start earning money to buy things. During our stay on base housing, the most exciting thing, for a few young kids that never had much to indulge on, was the ice cream man. Every evening, Monday through Friday, right as the sun was setting, we could expect to hear the jingle of his truck. Getting the money to treat ourselves from our parents was incredibly rare, so we'd sit around disappointed, watching our friends get to enjoy it. We hoped every night that the night after would be the next time we'd get to enjoy our share.

One day, as I was outside playing in the hot summer sun, I noticed someone had set out a few extra-large boxes by our street's dumpster. Curious, I walked over to see what treasures the boxes held. I was shocked to see that all of them were filled to the top with books that were still in great condition. A bookworm and avid reader since an early age, it was sad to see so many being tossed away. I knew my parents would never let me bring all of them home; I needed a creative opportunity to put them to use. There was no way I was going to let them just sit there in the condition they were in.

Then, a light bulb lit in my head. I knew exactly what I'd do with the books – I was going to sell them. I'd use the money afterwards to buy my siblings and I some ice cream with the cash I earned. I grabbed the boxes, nearly as tall as I was, and dragged them through our neighborhood apartments, going door to door. Lugging them up 4 flights of stairs, I pushed the burning in my arms to the back of my thoughts and forced myself to get to every neighbor. I was committed to selling these books. As the sun slowly started to set, I knew I needed to act fast to get enough money to afford the ice cream – they didn't come cheap. At 25 cents per book, I had to sell a little over ten just to buy one scoop. I ran across enough compassionate adults, who were quizzically intrigued by such a young salesgirl, that they turned over a few quarters to take some books off my load.

With each quarter, I became more and more ecstatic. We struggled to get much in life and here I was so close to getting what I was longing for, just by being willing to put in the work and sweat. I remember smiling from ear to ear when I finally heard the ice cream man pulling into our street. Counting the quarters, I had just enough to get us some for the night. Running up as fast as I could to be the first in line, giddy with excitement, I placed my orders and got the opportunity to enjoy two delicious scoops of cotton candy ice cream.

That was an eye-opening day for me. It would play a large part in the way I approached everything I wanted in life. It didn't matter that my family was poor and couldn't afford the finer things. If I was willing to get creative and put in the hard work, it'd pay enough to get me whatever I chased in life. I just had to pull my weight to make it happen. I realized, if I wanted it bad enough, I had to work hard to get it, and I was determined to get some ice cream. I held onto the books for a few more days, hiding them in the basement of our apartment building. I enjoyed a few more nights of my favorite flavors from the sale of the books. What I couldn't sell, I left in the basement to collect dust. A better fate, in my mind, than the dumpster.

Life led on like this for a couple of years, seeking and finding creativity in everything I saw and touched. It kept us out of the house and my mind off any tensions at home. We spent most days busy at school and when we got home and finished our homework, we spent most of the day playing outside. The less we stayed inside the less we got in trouble. This part of my life held the largest portion of happiness at any one period. Although it wouldn't last, it was enough to give me a slight glimpse into what life could be like, instead of what it had always been.

Living in Germany brought us closer to Turkey. My step-mother longed to see her own family again, so we made a trip out to visit her parents, now my step-grandparents.

They lived in a quaint little apartment home, decorated with a mix-match of floral and patterned rugs and furniture. I couldn't tell if they had an eccentric taste or if it was just an accumulation of random stuff bought through the years. They didn't live in the same city I had grown up in, the one my mother still lived in, so running into her was never a concern. We enjoyed getting to explore the new area and all the small ageing store fronts that littered the streets. Kids were running around laughing and playing with a worn-out soccer ball, while friends and family sat in front of shops, caught up in lively banter. The little town felt warm and homely.

I didn't know my grandparents very well and noticed that my step-grandmother was a small frail woman. She spoke in hushed tones and there was a gentleness to her demeanor. She also portrayed a delicate personality that seemed like it came from a lifetime of enduring pain. My step-grandfather was the complete opposite. From the moment I met him, I felt an intuitive level of unease towards him. So strong, that I sometimes felt queasy. Sitting across from him, I'd squirm under his beady gaze, longing to be anywhere but in his presence. I didn't have to sit far from him to smell the alcohol on his breath. The smell of it also lingered in the room; the walls seemed to be soaked in his foul liquor of choice. I'd find him usually drunk by mid-day, laughing belligerently at jokes he only seemed to find any humor in. When most people laugh, you join in on the laughter – or at least smile, by the shared joy of seeing someone so amused. When he laughed, I forced a smile, making an effort to hide my repulsion. I didn't understand why this strange man, I'd never met before, made my skin crawl.

It wouldn't be long before his dry sense of humor was directed towards me. One hot afternoon, feeling parched, I meekly asked him for a glass of water. He pointed in the direction of a glass sitting on the dining room table that was filled with a clear liquid. He nodded his head in its direction, implying that I should drink it, with a strange smirk across his face. Not privy to his childish game, I went over and took a large gulp. My throat seared in pain and I coughed up the ghastliest thing I had ever drunk in my life. Choking and in shock, I ran to the kitchen, desperately searching for a glass of water to wash away the alcohol. Cheeks flushed, I was livid listening to him bellow in laughter. *Only a fool would find it hilarious to trick a little girl into gulping down a mouthful of hard liquor*, I thought. Later in life, I'd come to realize how strong of an intuition I had towards people and how often that intuition was correct about their true character. Call it God, or inner wisdom, but I'd come to find out my instant disdain for him was warranted.

One evening, I sat on the couch watching T.V. while the rest of the family gathered outside. He came into the living room giggling in his drunkenness. Plopping down on the couch next to me, his leg grazed mine. I instantly felt the hair on my neck rise. An anxious laugh escaped my lips as he started running his hands down my back and brought it around to squeeze my thigh. He slurred through words, but I couldn't understand any of it. The alcohol on his breath burned my nostrils and I turned my head away from him. Scooching out of his touch, I tried making my discomfort evident. Before I could see his reaction, the door opened, and my parents made their way inside. Flooded with relief, I let out a quiet sigh.

This man was going to be a nightmare. I couldn't wait to leave and go back home.

2.

THE ABUSE

That evening I fell asleep on the living room couch while the rest of the family slept in separate bedrooms. I remember waking up late in the middle of the night, hearing an odd noise out in the hallway. I looked up with heavy eyes to see a figure in white heading towards the living room's glass door. I became frightened, thinking I was seeing a ghost. I covered my head with my blanket, willing it to go away. I didn't hear a thing after, and in my exhaustion, fell quickly back asleep. The next morning, I woke up in confusion, feeling an odd chill under the blankets. I lifted them up and glanced down to find that my pants and underwear had been removed and were gently tucked next to my legs. Perplexed and a little frightened, I ran the night over in my head, trying to remember anything out of the ordinary. Coming up short, I quickly threw the clothes back on, worried I'd get in a heap of trouble if my parents saw me in that condition.

I've struggled with memory loss my whole life. They say it's a common symptom when you've lived through traumatic events. Details and timelines get warped, but some moments were so awful, my mind has a hard time pushing them far enough away. I don't remember much about the first day I was sexually abused. I don't have any recollection of why I was home alone with my step-grandpa, and nothing of what had occurred prior to him dragging me by my arm into his bedroom. I just remember the sun shining through the curtains, so I knew it was daylight. I remember grabbing his hand to loosen the fingers that burned into my arm and looking up at him in alarm – unaware of his intentions, but aware he didn't mean well by them.

I tried digging my heels into the carpet, but it made no difference to the strength and determination he had. I cried out for him to stop, that he was hurting me, but it didn't slow him in his fight to get me into his bedroom. Once we reached it, he tossed me onto the bed and started ripping my pants and underwear off. I tried holding them up, praying for strength to keep him from taking them off my body. He slapped me so hard, my head spun, and small lights danced around the room. My hands fell to the side, my whole body going limp as he lifted my legs and pulled my bottoms off. I heard his pants lightly hit the floor and listened sickeningly as he grunted through the effort of taking his own underwear off. I shut my eyes, now soaked in tears, and looked away.

He shoved my legs in the air and pressed his member against me. I gasped in pain as he picked up speed and pressure, working himself into a sweat, his hands now moist on my ankles. I cried and felt like I was suffocating as he aggressively worked himself into a climax. As quickly as it had begun, it was over. He let my legs drop off the side of the bed, making my body jolt from the momentum. My eyes opened wide. My breathing was shallow and my whole body shivered, I felt chilled to my bones. What took only a few minutes felt like hours. My mouth was dry and heavy. "Hurry up and put on your clothes," he hissed in Turkish. "If you tell anyone about this, I'll have your dad beat you for shaming the family, do you understand?" I watched in quiet stillness as he yanked his clothes back on. Finally, I nodded. My eyes felt heavy, I wanted to curl up and fall asleep on the floor, and I felt a pressure on my chest that made it hard to breath. It was like my soul disappeared to another place in that moment, leaving behind a shattered body. Everything inside of me shut down and I listened as he barked out his demands to remain silent.

Unable to think, I slowly pulled my pants up, my hands shaking uncontrollably. I didn't know how to handle this, couldn't even register what had actually happened, but knew this monster had violated me. I didn't know how to react. I was terrified and in shock, and cleaned up after his mess as he ordered me around. The only thing my mind latched onto were his words repeating in a broken rhythm in my head. *If my dad found out about this, he would beat me.* I already lived everyday in fear of my father's anger, to know that I would be punished because of my step-grandfathers actions ate away at me. I did the only thing I knew how to do, I let my whole mind and body shut down, and removed any bit of emotion.

I walked out of his bedroom, feeling disoriented, and made my way into the living room. Curling up into the couch, tucking my legs underneath me, I stared at the T.V. I wrapped my arms tightly around my body, lost in a daze until my family made their way back home. My grandfather had stayed in his bedroom until then. I didn't pay him any attention as he started up a conversation with my parents. I was too afraid to greet my siblings, worried the moment my mouth opened that I'd hurl all over myself. I wanted to run scalding water over my skin to wash away the filth and grime that I felt covered me from head to toe.

I laid in bed that night, exhausted from the emotional breakdown I silently endured. I didn't know what to think or how to feel. I could still feel the burning in my arm from when he dragged me into his bedroom. I still felt the warmth of his member when he pressed it up against me. I shuddered thinking of the sensation of the liquid that covered my belly when he finished. Nausea washed over me in a thick wave and I ran to the bathroom and threw up.

It all made sense. The morning I woke up with my pants and underwear pulled off finally had some meaning behind it. He must've been spooked by something not to have slipped them back on. I probably stirred in my sleep or he heard someone moving around and took off to his bedroom before being caught. After that day in his bedroom, he became bolder in his advancements. Grazing against my backside or fondling my breasts while my parents were in the kitchen or in a neighboring room. Always giving me that knowing look that if I made a peep, it would be all over for me. I felt trapped.

"You'll shame your whole family, they'll never want anything to do with you," he'd say. I stared off at the wall, unwilling to meet his gaze as he fondled my body and whispered threats into my ear. My stomach would twist into knots in disgust and fear. My anxiety boiled over, my heart pounding, waiting for him to slip up and my parents to catch him in the act. Terrified that my father would beat me after finding out what was happening. I didn't quite understand what bringing shame on the family meant, but I knew what it meant to make my dad angry, so I begged and willed him, in my mind, to stop touching me before someone walked into the room.

One evening, only a couple of days before we were set to leave, we spent our time outside with the neighbors, enjoying a simple potluck. I stayed as close to my parents and siblings as I could that night, doing all I could to ensure I was never in a space alone with my abuser. I waited in anticipation for the day we'd leave, promising myself I'd avoid him at all cost. A few hours into the night and I had the urge to use the restroom. I held it in for as long as I could and knew I had to head to the toilet or I'd soil myself. I looked around and noticed my grandfather distracted in conversation. I quietly made my way inside, out of his line of sight, and tried not to draw any attention in my direction.

Parched from running around all night with my siblings, I stepped into the kitchen to quickly grab a glass of water, then made my way to the bathroom. Half way down the hall, I felt a hand press up against my lower back. My heart dropped into the pit of my stomach. I hadn't heard him come in, *why hadn't I heard him*, I yelled at myself. My heart began to race as he nudged me to pick up speed. Trembling, I continued slowly towards the bathroom, avoiding his persistence to get me in the confined space. I pleaded desperately to God, screamed for His help, and for all of this to stop. I begged Him to save me from this monster. I just wanted this to be over, my heart felt like it was bleeding. I heard him shut the door behind me and listened in despair as the lock turned and sealed us in.

The cry I was holding inside slipped out in a pathetic whimper. I felt the nauseating warmth of him on my back as he walked up and stood directly behind me. He fondled with his pants, struggling through his grunts. Finally, successfully getting them off, they dropped to the tiled floor with a soft thud. His belt clanged against the tile and echoed through the cold bathroom. My throat stung, my mouth felt dry again. I held my hands to the side of me, tightening them into a fist, willing my mind to escape this room and what was to come. He pulled my pants and underwear down, grabbed me and shoved me backwards into his half-naked body. I pressed a hand against my belly to keep from throwing up. Wrapping his hands around on chest, he squeezed my breasts till they burned in agonizing pain, then slid his hand down between my legs, to violate any essence of childhood I had left. He motioned his member back and forth into my backside. I shut my eyes tight and wanted to cover my ears against his heavy breathing. I felt his hot breath on my neck and wanted to curl up in a fetal position. I couldn't control the tears anymore – they flowed out in a silent cry, soaking my cheeks before dripping on the floor. I wanted nothing more than to die.

Unexpectedly, a knock came at the door, my eyes widened, and I whipped my head around towards the sound. He grabbed me as hard as he could and yanked me into his chest. I lost my breath with the impact. He tightly pressed his hand over my nose and mouth and quietly hissed threats into my ear to keep my mouth shut.

"Dad, have you seen Linda?" I heard my stepmother ask. "We can't find her anywhere."

"No, I haven't, I'm just using the restroom. I haven't seen her," he responded.

I felt both desperation for her to come in and save me but dreaded what would happen to me if she had. I went limp, consumed with despair, as I heard her footsteps lead her back outside. Fortunately, the moment had spooked him. Demanding I put my clothes back on, he hastily dressed.

"I'm going to leave the bathroom first, you stay in here and wait a while, and tell them you were laying down on the couch. If you tell them what just happened, your dad will beat you," he growled.

Unable to hide the disgust in my expression any longer, I scowled at him and nodded. As I buttoned my jeans, he walked out of the bathroom, closing the door shut. I slumped against the wall and slid to the floor. Putting my head in my hands, trembling in fury and loathing the scum disguised as a human, I prayed to God to let me die that day.

Later that evening, on a drive with my step-mother, she asked what had happened to me during that short time I was gone. Implying she wanted the truth about what *really* happened, instead of the scripted story I relayed by the demand of her father. I couldn't take the lies and abuse anymore. I made up my mind, I'd rather be beat over the shame I brought on the family than let that man go another day laying his hands on me. I told her everything. To my naïve astonishment, generally in the way that it goes with young children, I didn't get in trouble as I had expected. My parents were furious, but not at me. The beatings, I'd been sworn to, would never come. My parents discussed the whole incident with my step-grandmother and had me reshare the details of all that had occurred.

When my father confronted my step-grandpa, he made a feeble attempt to deny the abuse. But I could hear his voice break as I listened-in from another room, his lie evident to everyone. My father, fueled by absolute rage, beat my step-grandfather till screams for him to stop were echoed throughout the house. My brothers and I sat in another room with the door shut, hearing the screaming and yelling, and just stared at each other in horror. My step-grandpa was then taken to the emergency room in a cab. The overwhelming mixture of emotions left me drained. Fear and exhaustion turned into gratitude and relief. It was all over, he'd never lay a hand on me again.

Finally, we packed our bags and went back home. I spent weeks fighting nightmares and the awful memories plagued me. It would be a long journey before I found strength to emotionally heal from the abuse. I mostly got through it by shoving the memories far into the back of my mind, doing everything to forget that it even happened. If I wanted to move on, I couldn't let those memories keep resurfacing to haunt me. I had to leave it in the past and move forward. It wasn't until my little sister, Monica, was born, that I was able to find an exciting distraction to keep my mind off the worst of it. Our family had now grown to seven. On top of my brothers, I now had two beautiful sisters to cherish.

• • •

It took some time, but life finally found some sense of normalcy. I did what I could to keep my focus on school, friends, and hobbies. Eventually, the military took us back to Texas. To a new town called Del Rio, right near the border of Mexico. I knew I'd miss my life and friends in Germany, hating the move back to the States. Although you get used to moving around when you're in the military, it's never easy in the beginning. You're thrown into a new world with no friends and it seems nearly impossible breaking into a group that has built a bond since they were in Elementary. It didn't help that I was an incredibly shy and timid girl. I wore clothes that were far too big for me, my hair was long and pitch black – my brothers teased that I looked like the girl straight out of the "Ring" movie. I also had a really tough time with puberty and broke out all over my face. My own brothers dubbed me "pepperoni face." I had to love 'em, it was cruel but clever.

I didn't have nice clothes like the girls who I went to school with, didn't get to use hair products to be more in style, and didn't have the privilege of affording makeup to cover up the onslaught of blemishes and scarring from the pimples. School was tough. You'd think my dark Turkish features would pass me by well enough in a school with nearly 90% of the population being Hispanic, but instead, I was tormented constantly for being one of the few "white girls." The school "gangs" did everything they could to make the first few years of my life a living hell. I got into countless fights with girls I'd never even met. In Del Rio, when you got into a fight in school, you had to appear in court and would be fined if you were the aggressor. I'm sure the judge eventually began to count on me being a familiar face in his courtroom. Fortunately, I was never fined. My fights were in self-defense against a gang of girls I still didn't know by first-name. The fights finally stopped after I made a point that if I was going down, I'd take my aggressors down in a bloody mess with me.

I had a few close friends, but outside of that, high school felt lonely. Life in elementary and middle school In Germany was full of young kids exploring the world, finding creativity, and making friends with as many people as they could. It was a rare occasion to come across a bully in my other schools. At this school, it was rare to find someone who wasn't being an ass. Being kind seemed to be the exception at this place. Sure, everyone loved the popular kids, but I was at the bottom of the totem pole.

The loneliness was draining, smothering me in this small town. I felt alone at home and felt even more alone at school. Happiness between friends was always brief, disrupted by the ugliness and drama from other students. The depression inside took a turn for the worse. I was sinking into this bitter version of myself. I had always been good in school, bringing home grades my parents could be proud of, but my grades began to suffer. The tension at home grew worse in result of it. My parents didn't expect anything less than A's and B's, bringing a C or less meant some form of hard punishment. My depression was so heavy on my spirit, my grades started to drop into the D's and F's, something that was out of the ordinary for me. To avoid getting chewed out and punished, I learned how to create fake progress reports. I was lucky that our school didn't have the technology to share grades online, at that time. I loved schoolwork, I was great in all my classes, but lost the motivation to put in the work. Life didn't feel like it was worth living, so I stopped caring.

Homelife was incredibly strict. After school, we did homework, cleaned the house, ate dinner, and went straight to bed. Weekends were focused on excessive cleaning, and if we were lucky enough to have spare time, then we would get a momentary break to play with the other military kids that lived in our cul-de-sac. I was the oldest, so I received the brunt of the punishment if the house wasn't properly cleaned. Most of my free time was spent reading books when we were cooped up inside. It seemed most of our childhood was spent being grounded for one reason or another, so I found an escape in the stories I read.

We had a lot of fun with our friends when we got to hang out with them, but most of the days I felt isolated. I had my brothers and sisters, but they had their own interests that didn't blend with mine. Life at home got a little more exciting when my youngest sister, Jessica, was born. I was now the oldest of 6 kids. Before long, the excitement died down, and I was looking for a second outlet. Music was the next escape. I tuned out the loneliness with a playlist that included Panic at The Disco, Fall Out Boy, My Chemical Romance, 30 Seconds to Mars, and a few other bands that fell in the same genre and were popular among kids at that time.

I had been raised most of my life as a Muslim. My father's father was a Christian pastor, and aside from church visits we had with them, the church wasn't engrained into our home life. I started longing for a more meaningful relationship with God, in hopes that it would help me pull away from the sadness I felt every day. So, I decided to go to the small non-denominational church on base. My parents didn't attend, but I took my brothers with me a few times. I wanted them to experience their own relationship with God.

Church was my escape. It was the only place I went where I felt loved. The only place where I felt like I had a purpose. I joined the choir with a deep passion for singing and started to feel like I was truly a part of something. I began to grow a bond with God that allowed me to feel worthy of living. My parents never let me out to do much with friends, but for church events, they made an exception. Through that, I found an escape from the tension at home and school.

Whether you believe in God or not, He was the rock I leaned on for support. If it wasn't for Him and my belief in Him, I truly don't believe I would have gotten through those earlier years when suicide plagued me daily. If it wasn't for my belief in Him, I would have taken my life in my early teens. It was my love for Him and the love I felt from Him that helped me to hold on. I begged Him, I cried to Him, I grew a bond with God that I felt was unbreakable. I had this overwhelming feeling, even during my lowest days, that if I just held on, there would be something bigger in store for me in my future. That I could get out of that small town with a school full of people who hated me, from a home that I didn't feel like I belonged in, and from the continued abuse. I began to believe that life was full of so much potential and it gave me just enough assurance that it was worth not killing myself. I chose to hold on as strongly as I could. I held on through the growing depression and loneliness, and it was what I'd need to hold on through the next few years of continued sexual abuse.

I'm going to be honest with you, in the next part of my story, I'm going to lie to you. I've changed the name and identity of the person who spent the following 3 years molesting me. I had to change some of the scenarios and locations to hide the identity of the new monster I'd face in life. This isn't to protect the man who abused me, he lost that right the day he decided to touch me. Instead, it's to protect his family. If you've ever been a victim to abuse, you know there is more to us than just the victim and the predator. It's a spider web of connections to people that abuse affects, and so many get hurt when the truth comes out.

The man who abused me was a close relation to our family. He was married with young children of his own. I loved and adored his kids, innocent hearts who were shattered when they found out the true character of a father they loved. I feel incomplete telling my story by having to make this adjustment, but I will take this sacrifice to protect the identity of the innocent people hurt by the actions of one selfish man. No matter where this book ends up, it will follow them for the rest of their lives if the identity of their father is revealed, then broadcasted to people they know. It's unfair that they would have any form of negativity fall on their hands for actions they had no control of, but society will shame the whole family. I could have skipped telling you this part and just gone on with the story, but this has always played a large role in my pain. Going my whole life lying about the real name and identity of the man who abused me, to protect others. Although I spent years wanting his identity plastered across news outlets, wanting justice for the wrongs he committed, I kept his name off my tongue. Although he is no longer in a position to be a threat to society, I'll hide his real name in the book, to save his family's name, for now.

For the next 3 years, up until I was 16 years old, the man I'll rename as "Carl," molested me. I wish I could say that his molestation was as simple as a touch here, a grope there, or an inappropriate comment every once in a while. However, the things that man did to me and had me do to him will forever be a living nightmare. No matter how far I've come in life, there isn't any level of healing that could completely erase the memories of what he did to me. Carl did everything to me that should only ever occur between a husband and wife, or a consenting couple, aside from full penetration. Except we weren't husband and wife and there was never any double-sided consent.

He was a man in his early 30's and I was a young teenage girl. Puberty moved along quickly, and soon my body grew into a young woman's physique. There aren't enough words to explain to people the emotional roller coaster that abuse brings on. Made evident when they'd innocently ask why I didn't just go to my parents or to the police when it first started. The level of fear that paralyzes a child who goes through abuse doesn't provide sensible solutions to escape the situation. Did it change that I saw my own form of redemption when my father didn't end up beating me, but instead beat my step-grandpa who abused me the first time? No. Not in my mind, not at that age. This was an altogether different situation and different man, and I didn't know how to escape this version of a bad dream.

My relationship with my parents was strained, to say in the least. I felt a strong sense of hatred and contempt for the emotional and physical abuse they inflicted, themselves. I felt unloved at home. I felt bullied. I felt like I didn't belong. I didn't feel like I had a connection to them to find strength out of my depression and fear to tell someone what was going on. I was scared. Abuse, especially on a child, is so traumatic, that rational thinking isn't on the forefront of our minds. I became so paralyzed, by not only the fear, but also the confusion.

Why is this grown man touching me in this way? Why is this grown man telling me that this is alright, and it'll be fun when it feels like my insides are crawling and I feel like puking? Why is this happening again? Is there something wrong with me? These were the thoughts that replayed repeatedly. I couldn't rationalize what to do because, and despite my previous experience, sexual abuse was still a foreign concept for me to understand.

For years, as the molestation continued, I broke down inside. I felt like an empty vessel, used repeatedly for other people's pleasure, being raped of any pleasure of my own. I felt like the only person I had to run to, cry to, and beg for help from was God. I prayed, I screamed, I cried. I wanted desperately to find help but didn't know where to look for it. It felt like my life was in an endless loop of nightmares. I was bullied at school, felt hated at home, and lived in the shadow of my father's anger and my step-mother's disdain. Throw the sexual abuse on top of an already fragile child and there wasn't much hope left to live on.

The worst humiliation in my abuse didn't come from what was done to me, but what I was forced to do to my abuser. When your abuser tells you to take your clothes off and touch him, you do it in fear. When your abuser tells you to get on your knees and pleasure him with your mouth, you do it in fear. When he'd lay over my naked body, forcing me to watch him finish himself with his hands, I couldn't help but wonder what his wife thought he was doing in that moment. I wondered what his kids would think of him if they knew he was using his mouth to go down on a child so close to their own age. Everything except penetration. I stood, I laid, I sat. I was his toy for whatever fetish he had. I know these words might be hard to read, they're even harder to remember and write down. But it's important that you understand how awful my abuse was, so you can understand how triumphant my future success would be. Abuse is a horrific thing to endure, and we can't talk about it and make an impact in the world in reducing child abuse, by sugar coating what it is.

The only way to survive those moments was to escape. Since my body couldn't go anywhere, I escaped in my mind. I allowed it to get lost as far as it could go. I numbed my body from feeling any sensation through the abuse. I made up a fake world where there was magic, and I was the heroine. My body moved robotically to my abuser's demands, but I never came out of my own head. Sometimes, I stayed lost in my thoughts long after the abuse had ended, and I was back at home and in my room.

As a stubborn and hard-headed woman now, I struggled with my childhood self for just sitting there and taking the abuse instead of finding it in her to fight back. I had to learn that I wasn't a weak and pathetic child, just because in my petrified fear, I listened and obeyed the horrific things my abuser made me do. That's one of the hardest things you face as a victim. You feel pathetic. You know what's going on is wrong, you know you should say something, you know you should fight back and run, but as a child in that situation, feeling uncared for and unloved by everyone around you, you feel like there isn't an escape. Who would believe me? No one, I thought. This man that had a family, a strong reputation at work, no history of any form of abuse – who would believe *me* against him? I felt like there was no escape, no redemption this time around. This man was known by my family, he was close to them. No one would ever believe that this "good" man could ever do something so disgusting to a little girl, let alone for years. My step-mom had figured something odd was going on between my step-grandfather and I, because he had a history of abusing children. My abuser, now, was loved by nearly everyone who knew him. Surely, they'd think I was making this up for attention, I thought.

For me, depression is a physical thing. First it begins deep within you, then it starts to consume your whole being. It feels like a black tar that surrounds you, that only you can see. The more I struggled against it the deeper it pulled me in. They say depression is chemical, maybe for some people it is. My depression felt physical, it felt emotional. The horror in my life was real. My pain wasn't caused by a chemical imbalance, it was caused by the abuse, the emotional and physical torment, and the loneliness. The depression quickly built up thicker and thicker inside. When I wasn't feeling shattered and betrayed by the world, I felt furious that it stood by as a little girl was tormented.

"Why?!" I'd scream. "Why is this happening to me? Why are these people hurting me? I haven't done anything wrong, so why won't this pain go away?!"

I spent most of my nights crying myself to sleep. When I wasn't escaping to the made-up world in my mind, I was escaping into a new world in my books. I found strength through the stories, adding to my collection novels that depicted women who suffered through tragedies, only to turn it around and empower themselves. When I wasn't finding inspiration in the books, I was finding healing in the Bible. Getting to know God, talking to Him and asking Him over and over again to help me, gave me hope. I didn't have a religious connection to God, but instead, it was intimate and personal. I know not everyone believes in Him, I know most children don't even know who He is, but I knew Him, and He was all I had to lean on. Believing in Him was hope that escaping my pain was even a possibility. Even if people who had been through similar tragedies didn't believe in God, I hoped they had something to believe in that gave them the faith and courage to seek something bigger than our isolated suffering. A bigger meaning that says there is more to this world than what we see through our broken and teary eyes.

In my black tar of depression, a flame eventually lit. In that flame came a new kind of anger, and in that anger came determination. It was time to move on from this life, this abuse, and the belief that I was worthless. I was ready to escape, ready to fight, and ready to get away from it all. I would no longer let "Carl" harass my body and force me to do things to him. I'd no longer let the kids at school bully me into thinking I was nothing more than filth, and I'd no longer live in fear of my father and step-mother.

At 16 years old, after another day of being screamed at by my parents for an incident I no longer recall, I had finally had enough. That was the night I was going to turn a new chapter in my life and refused to endure the physical, sexual, and emotional abuse by the people who were closest to me. The small flame that burned within me started to grow brighter and it gave me a sense of power I had never felt before.

That evening, I stayed up long after everyone else had fallen asleep. I snuck my father's green military duffel bag out of a closet and began to stuff it with clothes and books. I hid my military I.D. card in my purse and tried to take whatever money I could find to get me by. I hid the bag in my closet and waited for the alarm clock to go off. The following morning, I got dressed for school and went through my usual routine. I waited for my father to leave for work before grabbing the bag out my closet and heading out the door.

I hurried to the bus stop, looking around nervously for my father's car, making sure it was nowhere in sight. I convinced my best friend and my brothers that I had a big school project in the bag and that I would show them what it was later that day. It's comedic to think about now. That bag was nearly my size and was bulging from how much stuff I had packed it with. In my naivety and passion for my books, I had filled it with nearly all my favorites. It wouldn't be long before I realized I'd made a mistake with how many I brought.

I hopped on the bus and watched in anxiety and excitement as it drove us out of the military base and towards school. As we pulled up to our usual drop off point, we all got off and I watched as everyone else walked towards the school buildings. I turned around and watched as the bus driver pulled off, quickly glancing down the street to see if any other buses were coming. I had to convince my best friend Katherine to go on without me to the courtyard, promising that I would have an explanation for my odd behavior later that day. It took a bit of convincing, but I finally got her to believe my lie and leave.

I waited till she was out of sight, surveyed the bus drop area to make sure no one else could see me, then knew it was time to say goodbye. I whispered a quick prayer about how much I loved my siblings, begged God to look after them and give them an amazing life and apologized about lying to my best friend. I grabbed my Walmart pre-paid phone out of my pocket, pulled out the battery, tossed it into the bottom of the green duffel bag and began to walk towards the highway.

3.

THE RUNAWAY

I ran away that day. Well, they call it running, but I could barely walk with the weight of the duffel bag slowing me down. I headed in the direction of the highway, taking backroads with no sense of where I was heading. I got turned around often and found myself lost in neighborhoods I'd never been through before. Eventually, I made my way through it all and finally got to the highway.

Walking along the edge of the road, I did my best to look inconspicuous, but didn't seem to do a very good job at it.

A scrawny little 16-year-old girl, walking along on the open road with a massive bag on her back, did nothing more than draw unwanted attention. I had no idea where I was going, the road ahead looked like it led to a place without civilization, but I made my way the best I could.

Despite a newly revived determination, the anxiety was still insufferable. I had intentions of going up north to Indiana to visit my grandparents on my father's side but had no real idea how I'd get there. Although I had always felt alone, it was an overwhelming sensation not to have my brothers and sisters nearby. I was already missing them terribly and started to choke up. I couldn't cry, I wouldn't.

As thick puddles of tears welled up on the corner of my eyes, I noticed a car pull up next to me. An old man with a toothless grin stared at me in a such a predatory and familiar manner, that it took me straight back to the memories of my step-grandfather's face. From the wrinkles, to his parting hairline, and even how he garbled his words. He was a near replica of the monster from my past. I instinctively stood up straight, lifted my chin, and stared him straight in the eyes. I felt a prickle of fear shoot up my spine, but I wouldn't let this man see it. I had left home to escape abuse, I would not be taken advantage of by a stranger on the side of the highway. The fear I felt fueled my anger and strength. My hands holding the duffel strap tightened in their grip.

"Do you need a ride?" he slurred.

I gritted a smile through my teeth. I could smell the alcohol in his car.

"No, I'm fine, I'm actually meeting up with my boyfriend here in a moment."

An odd lie for a girl in an odd location, but I stared directly back at him, without so much as a blink. I tried willing him to leave in my head. He insisted driving me to where I needed to go. It wasn't even a question that if I got into that car with that man, he wouldn't be taking me anywhere I *wanted* to go.

A car drove past us and it seemed to frighten him as he jerked his head in its direction.

"I'm fine," I repeated, impatiently. Trying to showcase my frustration that he had halted my travels. "I'm meeting up with someone here shortly, thanks anyways."

Before he could say anything else, I turned and continued walking in the direction I was originally heading in. He sat still in his car, not moving it back onto the road. I could feel the hair on my neck stand on end as I felt his gaze digging into my back. *Don't you dare get out of your car*, I thought. *Don't you dare. I don't care if I die here today, but I'll take you with me if you try anything.* I wasn't afraid. For the first time in my life, I felt courageous. The type of courage that comes in a flight or fight situation. I was already fleeing from the worst of my past, if this man made me fight for my life, I would fight without hesitation. As more cars drove by, I finally heard him pull back onto the main road and watched as he slowly drove past and kept going, only picking up speed just as he left my line of sight.

My shoulders drooped. The weight of how ugly the situation could have turned sat heavily on my mind. My sense of relief didn't last for long. My fear took on a whole new meaning, when a few minutes later, a Sheriff pulled over onto the side of the road and rolled his window down.

"Are you alright, where you off to?" He asked, smiling politely.

I knew my expression had given my nervousness away, so I appreciated his kindness. I swallowed the heavy lump in my throat and told myself not to give anything else away.

"Oh, I'm fine," I said in a false cheer. "Just doing a small hike."

"Hiking along the side of the highway?" he asked, puzzled.

I forced a laugh, "Yes, I know it's odd, but I hike as a hobby and plan to meet someone in the next town over."

"Alrighty then, how old are you?"

"18," I replied, standing my ground and willing myself to look straight into his eyes, praying he wouldn't ask me for my I.D. card.

"Well, just be careful out there, are you sure you don't need a ride anywhere?" He said, smiling, but I saw the strong questioning gaze in his eyes that said he didn't quite believe my story.

"Oh, yes absolutely, I'm perfectly fine, I do this all the time!" I added, smiling bigger and brighter.

I let out a sigh of relief when he finally seemed convinced and pulled off the side of the road and drove away. On the opposite side of the road, I recognized the black beat up car with the same old man, who stopped me earlier, driving by. His car slowed as he drove past. I glared into his driver side window, unable to see his face clearly, and scowled. I wouldn't let this man scare me, I was on my way to escaping a lifetime of nightmares, I'd do anything at this point to ensure nothing would stop me. His car picked up speed and that was the last I saw of him.

My back began to ache from the weight of the heavy bag, I was exhausted. I didn't have any food or water on hand and didn't see any type of gas station or shop nearby. I felt my anxiety increase and felt foolish for not being better prepared. I was in such a rush to get out of the house that morning, without being seen by anyone, that I ended up forgetting a few essentials. Although I wasn't regretting my decision, I was nervous of what was to come and wasn't sure how far I'd make it.

Then, I saw the dogs. Five of them in total, out here in the middle of nowhere, on the side of the road, without anyone nearby to claim them. They looked massive, wild, and hungry. I grew up with dogs, I was never afraid of them, but I was terrified of these ones. I had heard stories of dogs attacking people before, and knew if anything, these weren't the petting kind. There was a small hump of land a few feet away, with a large tree at the top of it. I made my way up the hill and sat behind the trunk of the tree and watched in nervousness as the dogs sniffed around and finally disappeared into thick shrubs.

An hour had passed and nothing stirred. I knew I was in the clear, but I couldn't will myself to get up. I was exhausted, weak, and felt broken. Suddenly, I was overcome by the years of emotions I had let well up inside. I cried so hard, my chest ached. I missed my siblings and wished my life wasn't such a tragic mess. I wished life had been easier, that things had been more normal so that I wouldn't be lost here in the middle of nowhere by myself. I begged God to help me, to give me a chance for once in my life, to find an opportunity for happiness.

I opened my duffel bag, took all the books out, and laid them on the grass. I was heartbroken knowing I had to leave them behind. The weight was unbearable, and I knew I wouldn't get very far if I kept dragging them along. I loved those books, they were my motivation and encouragement. I held on to the two I cherished the most and kept my Bible, as well. After a long cry and a few punches into the ground to let out my frustration, I finally found the strength to get back up and keep going. I knew I had to make it somewhere safe before it became dark. I had no idea how many hours had gone by. I needed to get off this long stretch of empty highway before my parents realized I wasn't coming home. Before the police started their search for me.

Another hour had passed before I was stopped by a red car pulling over in front of me. *Ugh, what now*, I thought. I walked up towards the car's passenger side, making sure to keep a good distance. The driver was a man who looked to be in his late 20's. Blonde with gray eyes, his eyes seemed to carry a twinkle. He ducked his head to get a better look at me and a smile teased at the corners of his lips.

"You need a ride?" He asked.

I was desperate, I knew I needed some help. I looked at him, then at his car, trying to make sense of his personality. He didn't seem threatening, he seemed normal, whatever that meant.

"What's in your duffel bag," he laughed, "you're not going to try to kill me, are you?"

I laughed, lowering my guard as I realized how nutty I must have looked myself. "I should be asking you the same thing," I responded. "Yeah, I could use a ride if you don't mind. I'm a bit exhausted from walking."

"Sure thing, hop in." He threw open the passenger side door.

I walked up to the door, threw my bag into the backseat and slipped into the passenger seat. Now I know you're probably thinking, Linda, what the heck are you doing getting into a strange man's car after all you've been through? It's difficult to explain, but I felt intuitively that this man truly could help me, that he wasn't anything to be concerned about. Fortunately, I ended up being right. Chris was in Texas because of work, brought out this way from Ohio, to handle a few branch meetings throughout the southern region. He held some sales position for Home Depot and was now heading a few towns over for his next meeting. I had him convinced that I was 18 years old, out hiking for the heck of it, and that I had gone through my money faster than I had intended. I shared with him that I was on a hike to Indiana and wasn't sure how I was going to get there since I had been through all my resources.

He agreed to help drive me as far up north as he could and would buy me a bus ticket to Indiana from there. In that time, he let me stay in his hotel with him and took care of me for the next couple of days. I felt so incredibly relieved that I was finally heading in the right direction, even more grateful I was finally getting some help.

One evening, when Chris was at work, I went outside to go for a walk in the cool evening air. I loved going for walks at night. It always helped me feel connected to nature, which in turn, helped me feel relaxed and cleared my mind. On the opposite side of the parking lot sat an odd-looking structure. On 6 stone pillars sat a roof, the whole structure was maybe about 5 feet tall. It had been tarnished by some graffiti and most of the shingles were crumbling. It was the oddest thing I had ever seen, sitting in the most random location. I climbed on top of it and laid there, staring up at the night sky. I was mesmerized by how pitch black it was and the number of stars that seemed to stare back at me. It was breathtaking. I soaked in the sounds of this strange corner of the world. People were caught up in an excited conversation in the distance, vehicles buzzed by, and the night was filled with the sound of frogs and crickets. The North Star caught my eye, I loved how it stood out despite the millions of other sparkling stars in the sky. She was always present, guiding people home for thousands of years. It felt like a sign and I embraced it.

A calm breeze lightly blew my hair, and as it gently lifted the strands, it also lifted my spirit. When I closed my eyes, I felt like I was floating in a distant world, and I wanted to lay there forever. I had never in my life experienced such a welcoming sense of peace and longed to never lose that freeing encounter. I thanked God for allowing me to catch a break and pleaded that He'd guide my journey on. I had no idea where I'd be heading in this life but wished that He'd always be there to direct me. I knew deep down, that one day, I'd build a life that was incredible and worth living. Knew that I'd marry a wonderful man, have children I'd spoil with undying love, and finally learn what real happiness was all about. That was the first night I ever thought about writing a book and telling my life story. It was then, I decided I'd work hard to build my own business empire and find personal healing, in hopes that I'd share my story with the world. I knew I wanted to connect with others that had gone through the same things I had been through and wanted to build a life that could encourage them to persevere. Before I could do that, I had to figure out how I could turn my story around to becoming one that was motivational and inspirational. I needed something solid to encourage others that happiness was a possibility, no matter how hard our struggles were to overcome. Nearly 10 years later, I finally would have the opportunity to fulfill the promise I made myself that night. I'd finally get to put my story on paper and share with others how I escaped my nightmare and went on to conquering big things.

Three days after I had run away, I hopped onto my emails, and noticed a message from my father. He asked where I was and begged that I come back home, stating that the whole family was distraught because of my disappearance. Rumors had spread around at school that I had run away with some boyfriend, I didn't even have a boyfriend, and rolled my eyes at the things people were making up. I messaged back and told him I was alright, that I couldn't tell him where I was, but I was heading to go see my grandparents. Pleading again for my location, he promised he'd come up to help me do whatever I needed and wouldn't force me to come back home.

My emotions got the best of me and I broke down to Chris and told him everything. I told him I was only 16 years old, that I'd run away from home, and now my parents were trying to find me. Surprisingly, he wasn't upset about the situation and talked me through it to decide what I wanted to do. I continued to communicate with my father via email, then transitioned to conversations with him on the phone. I refused to get into the details of why I ran away. I still felt disconnected from him and had no intentions of telling him anything. I held firm on my plans, refusing to go home, but instead would still be heading to Indiana.

Assuring me he had no problem with that, he added that he only wanted to come up and get my bus ticket for me, give me some money, and make sure I was on my way safely. Agreeing, I met with him a few hours later at a Denny's. I knew he wanted to talk but I remained quiet and distant. We went to a local Greyhound station, he picked up a ticket for me to head to Indiana, then handed me some cash to take care of my needs until I got there. I could tell he wanted to ask more questions, but didn't say anything more than a goodbye, seeming to understand the gap in our relationship and the reason I pulled away from him. After an awkward hug and a goodbye, I hopped on the bus to Terre Haute, Indiana. I called Chris on the way, thanking him for his help and letting him know I was finally heading to my destination.

• • •

I met up with my grandparents the following day and they brought me into their home with loving arms. They knew something was wrong but gave me enough distance to talk about it when I was ready to. I started school in

Terre Haute and lived a comfortable life at my grandparent's home, getting used to the routine of things, and finally finding some peace away from the abuse. Finding friends at school was a little tough, but eventually, I had a crowd of my own to spend time with during lunch breaks. I started dating a Senior, and had a blast attending his prom, my first one, ever. I dressed up in a beautiful lace ivory gown and felt like a normal girl for once in my life. His family came from good money, so we enjoyed each other's company, and I got the brief chance to know what it was like to be spoiled.

For the first time in my life, I finally started to feel normal. As with all good things in my life, this would be another phase that wouldn't last. This new life, that I thought would be my opportunity to start all over again, began to crumble. The laughter and enjoyment disappeared, like a lighter had been taken to the corners of my life and burned the happy image away. It didn't matter how nice life felt on the outside, on the inside, I was still broken and depressed. I missed my siblings, and although I found comfort in this new life, I didn't feel at home.

Then, one day, the truth came out about my abuse. On a drive with my grandpa, we started talking about my struggles and I confessed to the sexual abuse I had run away from. My grandparents were familiar with the man who molested me. Telling the truth for the first time, after years of hiding it inside, felt like the most relieving, yet terrifying, thing I had ever done. Afterwards, I had no idea how it would all pan out, but I begged them not to tell anyone or say anything and hoped that it would all just disappear. I just wanted the relief of sharing what I had suffered through alone, then wanted to move on from it, never having to address it again. Unfortunately, that's not how it panned out. Soon, close family members heard about the abuse I had gone through. Things fell apart even more when my parents were called and were addressed with the claims I was making.

I guess I should have expected people to think of me as a liar, but it still hurt nonetheless. I was accusing a man, who the family knew and adored, for sexually abusing me for years. I was the crazy 16-year-old teenager that ran away from home, why would I be telling the truth? Except for my grandmother and a couple of aunts that lived nearby, no one else truly believed me. They said they did, but their actions and attitude said otherwise. The atmosphere in the house completely shifted, and I felt even more isolated in my pain. When "Carl" was finally confronted by the family, it went as expected, he denied it ever happened. My grandparents had him on speaker phone when they called, so when I heard the words come out of his mouth that I was making things up - I screamed and cried, exploding in anger and frustration. I ran up to my room, slammed the door, and hated Carl for being an absolute coward. To have gone through years of the horror that I had gone through, only to have my pain minimized by his denial of the incidents. Even though I always thought a man like that would never admit to his wrong doings, hearing him deny everything to my family left me feeling lost. Nothing hurts more than being the victim of your own tragedy, only to be looked at by everyone as if you were the bad guy.

The nightmare I had thought I had escaped from was now in front of me, all over again, but the pain was different this time. I was completely humiliated. I had always wanted to hide behind my dirty secret, never wanted to tell anyone how broken and abused I was, it was such a hard thing to talk about. But everything I had ever felt went out the window because Carl said he was innocent. I decided than that I'd leave my grandparent's home and go off on my own. I hated people, no longer trusted anyone, and felt so betrayed. I prayed for guidance as I made plans in my mind for my next escape.

Only a couple of days later, my grandma shared with me the most unexpected news. Carl, I guess by his own guilt, confessed. To everything! Yes, you read that right, he confessed! As awful as the whole experience had been, I was beyond ecstatic by the news. Finally, I was being justified. Redeemed, even. Years of abuse and hiding

71

behind it for fear of no one believing me - the truth had finally come out. But that excitement wouldn't last long.

As a survivor of abuse, I learned that people *not* believing me wasn't the hardest thing to go through. The hardest part of it was the people who *did* believe me, that then treated me differently because of it. That's how it played out. I thought things would get better, but they got worse. I loved my grandparents dearly, they took me in and helped me in a time of need, but I couldn't help but get the sensation that I was the black sheep in the family. That I was the broken one. That I was so destroyed by what had happened, there was this expectation from everyone that I would somehow turn out crazy. But I wasn't crazy, I was depressed. I didn't want to turn to drugs or alcohol or some wild life that everyone expected from me. I just, for once in my life, wanted to live in a stable house and feel normal like everyone else.

The mood in the house brought my depression back in full force. I felt alone and lost all over again. Again, my grades started to plummet, and I was getting in fights at school. My emotions got the best of me when I heard two girls trashing my name, and when I went to confront them, one of them slapped me and I lost all awareness of my surroundings as the whole world went red. Coming out of it, I remember being dragged away and would later find out that one of the girls ended up being hospitalized.

Even though they laid their hands on me first, and the whole fight felt justified as self-defense, my grandparents were furious with me. The school discussed kicking me out for good or suspending me. I thought everything was such a joke. I get slapped in the face, but I get the crap end of everyone's reaction just because I made a point that no one would ever get away with hitting me again. My grandpa no longer wanted me to stay with them, but instead wanted me to go back to my parent's home. It felt like everyone turned against me. By my grandfather's own admission, he no longer wanted me there, afraid I'd make claims he was inappropriately touching me. Even after Carl had confessed, I was still being treated like I was the one going around making up stories about people. I had run away from the monsters and a life that nearly broke me and here I was being sent back to it. Words can't explain the intense mixture of anger and sadness that brewed inside. It overwhelmed me, and with my head hung low, I took a bus back to the home I had thought I left behind. Feeling unloved, unwanted, ashamed, and used - I felt like I had nothing to live for.

Now back home in Texas, things didn't go over well and began to unravel only shortly after I came back. I was betrayed and dumped by the people in my life who were supposed to love me, but instead turned me away, because they thought that I "might" turn into a problem. I had searched for help and guidance, but in their own fear, I was shut out.

I couldn't even tell you what the argument was the day I left home again. I remember getting into a big fight with my step-mom and for the first time in my life I yelled back at her. I didn't care anymore, infuriated and dumped back into a life that brought me back so close to the abuse I had left, I was ready to leave this disastrous life and just be alone. I didn't want to rely on anyone anymore, I'd just get turned away or treated like I had some kind of disease. I had survived alone so far, I'd continue surviving without anyone's help.

I packed my bags and left again. This time, I headed to Oklahoma, to meet up with a guy I had met online. I ended up staying in Oklahoma for a few months, in a small little town in the middle of nowhere. Drew lived with his mom and his sister, so I bunked with them in their tiny little house. I thought we had lived border line poverty before, this experience was definitely under the poverty line. Shortly after realizing I wasn't really in love with him, but using him to fill the void and loneliness, I felt guilty and called the relationship off. He didn't take it so well and burned all of my things. I stayed in the area and bounced from one boyfriend to another, doing what I could to keep from feeling alone. I benefited from them by having a place to stay, but none of the relationships lasted. I felt desperate in them, and in that desperation, I felt gross. Ending all of them before they'd get too far.

Months had passed, and I had word that my parents had moved to San Antonio. I decided to go visit them in their new home. I was missing my siblings and was tiring of limited opportunities available in a small town with one tiny grocery store. I knew going back home would feel incredibly uncomfortable, but I needed some stable ground to find a new direction to head in. Once I got to San Antonio, I ended up staying with my parents for a couple of months. I got a job at a Chic Fil A and moved out into a small apartment complex nearby, shortly thereafter.

I didn't have a car and walked back and forth to work every day. I struggled with my low minimum-wage income, hardly able to keep up with my measly rent, utilities, and groceries. So, I had to get a second job at a Mexican restaurant to keep afloat. Life went down the shoot all over again when the restaurant burned down from a crazy kitchen accident. I couldn't get another job that paid well enough to sustain my bills and was still in walking distance to my apartment. I tried dumb tactics to make some money, like throwing a beer party in my tiny studio apartment and charged a door fee. You'd be surprised, as well as I was, how many people showed up and paid. But it still didn't get me enough to pay the now overdue rent, and my apartment was destroyed by drunks. I listened in horror as someone puked all over the bathroom floor, smelled the disgusting pee all over my rugs, and noticed the holes in the doors and walls. All around me were drunk passed out teens, I couldn't help but look at them in disgust. I was sober and never could understand why anyone would willingly drink something so foul as beer to only be left in such a blubbering condition. For someone who never drank, I seemed to throw a pretty good party for a bunch of alcoholic teenagers.

This time I wasn't angry at anyone else but myself and my own bad luck. I just felt like I couldn't catch a break. I took what little money I had and went to a Target. I bought a tent and some camping supplies and walked to the closest forest I could get to, pitched up my tent and decided this is where I'd live from now on. I say forest, but that area didn't produce much more than small patches of thick trees and shrubs, it wasn't like the mountains in Washington. Abandoning my apartment with most of my personal belongings, aside from a few necessities, I took what I needed and decided to start this new life in my tent. I quit Chic Fil A after another bad breakup with a boyfriend who worked there, I really was on a roll with these relationships, and started a part time position at a pizzeria.

Here I was, working at a pizza joint for minimum wage, and living out of a tent in the middle of some thick shrubs in San Antonio, Texas. Life was really starting to shape up for me...

4.

HOMELESSNESS

Living in a tent is as glamorous as it sounds. The days were hot and blistering and the nights were chilly. After work, I'd spend any free time walking to the nearby Borders to dive into all of their books, fiction and non-fiction. I fell in love with the fantasy side of stories but was also inspired by the tips and advice from non-fiction novels that went over building a business empire. I was determined that one day, I'd find a creative enough path to build one on my own.

I slept on the floor of my tent. No matter how hard I tried to clear out the ground my tent sat on, I always woke up sore and could feel where a new rock had jabbed me through the night. Sleeping on the hard ground every night felt back breaking. One day, I found an abandoned mattress by a dumpster near an apartment complex, that still looked to be in good condition. In my desperation to stop the back pain, I waited till the middle of the night and dragged the mattress back to my tent. I cleaned it, as well as I could, before sleeping on it. It did feel a little gross the first few nights, but I had to put away my germaphobia, so I could finally get a good night's rest. Even at 17, sleeping on a bed of rocks and dirt starts to wear on the body. Texas isn't any stranger to spiders, either. The most anxiety-filled part of my stay was waking up every morning to spiders crawling around in my tent, and even in my bed. Sharing my bed with brown recluse spiders led to some massive paranoia.

I ate as much as I could at the pizzeria that I worked at, hid whatever leftovers I could fit into my purse. This was always my main meal on the days I worked. There weren't many restaurants in walking distance from where I was staying, so on the days I didn't work, I'd stock up on frozen foods and sandwich material from Target. I learned quickly how useless a candle is when you try to use it to cook food, even more useless when you're trying to heat frozen chicken patties one night when you're starving. From then on, I tried sticking to pre-made packaged goods. It wasn't the greatest, but I tried to find nutrition in whatever I could, treating myself to chocolate bars to keep some sense of sanity. I spent most of my days working, my afternoons at the book store, and my evenings reading by candle light. I spent most of my time re-reading my favorites, since I couldn't afford many new books.

I had built a consistent routine in my daily activities. I purchased a camping shower and toilet to maintain my hygiene. The pizzeria I worked at was connected to a dollar store, so I'd purchase 2 gallon jugs every day to use for drinking and keeping clean. Homeless or not, I'd never let anyone know, I had too much pride for that. Keeping clean and well-dressed was a must. For everyone on the outside looking in, they would have no clue about the lifestyle I was living. I wanted it to stay that way. No one needed to know a 17-year-old girl was living all by herself in the woods.

I love beautiful things and I love being surrounded by beauty, broke or not. To find pleasure in my living situation, I decided to spruce up the area I was staying in to make it feel a little cozier. Just because I was homeless didn't mean it had to feel that way. I started to work around my tent by clearing dead shrubs and broken tree limbs, even went so far as making a pathway to my tent with rocks and flowers. Yes, silly, I know – but it was encouraging to put some work into where I lived. I wanted to find beauty in every aspect of my life, no matter how many of those nights I fell asleep in tears. It kept my hands busy, which kept my mind busy, and in turn, helped me focus away from the depression.

I had a rough experience one day when I was clearing some shrubs from the back of my tent and I lost my footing and fell into a dead one. I screamed as one of the twigs went straight into my arm. In a panic, I pulled the stick out and pressed my hand against the open wound tightly, to help stop the bleeding. I ran into my tent and grabbed a bottle of alcohol and poured it over the wound and wrapped it with a shirt to help stop the blood.

Unfortunately, a few days later, my arm started to look worse. I could tell that a few pieces of the twig had broken off in my arm and had caused an infection. The wound looked yellow and was filled with puss, my arm now inflamed and swollen. Homeless, without a dime to spend on a doctor visit, I did what I thought best. I poured some alcohol into a cup and let my camping knife sit in it for a few minutes. Then, biting into a hand towel, I used the knife to cut the wound open and cleaned out the puss. To say the pain was excruciating is an understatement. I had to take the process slowly to see through the tears. I cleaned out the wound until the blood that flowed from it seemed clear and used a tweezer to pick out all the broken pieces. I closed my eyes and clamped down on the rag as hard as I could, and poured more alcohol over the now open wound, wrapped it tightly, and kept it dry. It finally healed well. I could tell I hadn't taken everything out of my arm, but it was finally healing nicely.

I was starting to get used to this life. Getting used to making my surrounding area beautiful, learning to live in solitude and simplicity. As hard as it is to be homeless, there is also an overwhelming sense of freedom attached to it when you no longer have to worry about all of the bills that need to be paid. If there was anything I could expect at this point in my life, it was the never-ending moments of bad luck. The first odd incident was the morning I woke up to my tent flap being zipped wide open. I had a pretty strict routine to my evening "home" care and couldn't for the life of me imagine leaving the thing wide open. I wasn't overly exhausted the night before and went to sleep reading a book. There was no way I could have been that oblivious. I was a little spooked.

After work, I bought a small hatchet axe and a mini lock from the store. I used that lock on my zippers every night to make sure I didn't wake up to it being zipped open again. I even stayed up late for a few nights, expecting for someone to come back and try to get into my tent, but no one came. The area I was in wasn't frightening during the day, but at night, it became a little creepy. Every small animal that rustled against the leaves sounded like heavy footsteps coming towards my tent. I worried about a police officer discovering me and giving me the boot, or a homeless man stumbling across me with bad intentions.

A few days later, after an exhausting work day, I walked the 30-minute trek back "home" to my tent. When it got into my line of sight, I dropped to my knees, defeated. Where my tent had sat for the past couple of months was now tattered remains of what it had once been. Someone discovered it and cut the tent to shreds. The whole place had been ransacked, what little I had was turned into a pile of mess. I just sat on the ground crying. It didn't matter what I was trying to do, or how strong I was trying to be, something was always there to disrupt it. I got up off the ground and walked to my tent to see what I could salvage. I felt sick to my stomach when I noticed my I.D., social security card, and birth certificate were missing. Slowly, the tears dried, and I swallowed the lump in my throat. My sadness turned into fury.

"ENOUGH!" I screamed. "ENOUGH! Why can't I ever catch a damn break??!!" I yelled at the world.

I flipped over my mattress and grabbed the blade I had hidden underneath it, noticing my axe missing. I switched it open and went out to find the people that ruined what little I had left in my life. The sun was already starting to set, and I knew I needed to figure out what I was doing before then. I'd have no where to go or sleep. Fueled by anger, I went in search of the culprits, finding them only a short five minutes later. I heard laughter and excited talking and knew instantly these were the fools that had ransacked my place. I made my way around the corner of the tree line, my knife in hand, ready to confront them.

As soon as I turned the corner, my hand holding the knife dropped to my side and I just sighed in frustration. My anger quickly turned to annoyance. I had five younger siblings, I got used to kids and their stupid decisions. What I had assumed were grown adults ended up being a bunch of kids who were no older than 8 to 12 years old. *For crying out loud*, I hissed in my thoughts.

"Alright, did you guys rip up that blue tent in the woods?" I yelled. I tried intimidating them by making my frustration obvious. I felt a little bad when they looked petrified, seeing me come out of nowhere with a knife in my hand. I closed the blade and put it into my pocket. "Well, was it you guys?" One of the little boys, who looked to be around 9, nodded his head yes. "Well that was my place guys, and you completely destroyed it and took my stuff." Another one of the kids seemed to find his courage and spoke up.

"Oh, we didn't know who lived there, we thought it was some crazy murderer that lived in there."

"Well, you should be glad that I wasn't some crazy murderer with how easy it was to find you guys. What you did wasn't cool at all. I need my stuff back that you took from me."

They apologized profusely and lead me towards the apartment complex they lived in and waited with me outside as one of them went in to get my stuff. When he came back out, he also had brought some food, water, and duct tape.

"We'll help put the tent back together," he offered, sheepishly.

I laughed. Kids had a great way of being a pain, only to turn it around and make you feel guilty for even getting upset in the first place. All of my frustration and anger dissipated in that moment. They took and destroyed what little I had, but they were kids, doing foolish things – not evil people.

"Sure, thank you," I said, "and thanks for the food."

As we walked back to my tent, I told them about my life in the woods and they were captivated. We all did our best to put the tent back together with duct tape, but I knew it wouldn't last for long. The boys came often to visit, bringing me food and water, and I was grateful for their company. They talked about school and home life and I taught them some camping tips and tricks. Although

I've long forgotten their names, I've never forgotten their faces. I hope they grew up to become better men from their experience with the homeless girl in the woods.

It was through the first rough thunderstorm that I realized my tent was pretty much a goner. The whole floor of the tent flooded, and I sat soaking wet on my mattress and just sighed in frustration. I rolled my eyes and just stared up at the ceiling of my tent and watched the water pour in like a waterfall. As comfortable as my short stay was, I knew I had to figure out how to move on and grow, and this was a big sign for that. I used what money I could save up to buy cheap motel rooms every now and then, walking an hour to get to the closest one. Sleeping on a real bed and showering in a real bathroom, even using a real toilet, was just the right amount of modern amenities to keep my sanity in tack. I now had to start brainstorming what direction to head in life. After doing a little research on my phone, I decided I was going to travel the world while working on a cargo ship.

One afternoon, laying on my bed in the tent, I pulled open my pre-paid cellphone and decided to hop on Facebook. I wasn't actively using it then, just hopped on occasionally to make teenage complaints about the world. I saw an unread message and noticed it was from an uncle I had met in my earlier years, at a family reunion in Tennessee. He was the youngest brother of my grandmother who passed before I was born, whose namesake I carried on. He felt a bond through that and decided to reach out when word had spread about my abuse and disappearance.

Excited to have made a family connection from a fond distant memory, we began chatting and I let him know about my circumstances. I shared my plans to work and travel around the world till I could grow deeper roots someday. He asked if I would be willing to visit Nashville and stay with them for a little while until I was better prepared with my future plans. He wanted to get me out of the tent and motels and find security in a stable home. After some convincing, he paid for my stay in a hotel for a few more nights, while making the arrangements to bring me up to Nashville. I was excited but guarded, as expected. Excited that someone, a family member no-less, wanted me around in their lives, even *after* they had heard the things I had been through. I was also guarded because I didn't really know them well and was worried about their expectations of what I'd do once I got there. My uncle threw out the idea of going to college, but at that time, my heart was pretty set on working on ships and travelling. I had a hard time living with people and worried it would cause issues. Living under someone else's house rules brought back too many memories of being controlled and it felt suffocating. But I felt like I was in a desperate enough position to give living with them a try. I packed what little I had, threw out my shredded tent and camping supplies, and prepared for a new adventure.

Coming to Nashville was the best decision I have ever made in my life. Even though there would be a few more hurtles to face, it was finally a step in the right direction. Moving in with my aunt and uncle, and their two beautiful daughters, was an exciting transition. They helped me learn how to drive a car, gave me one for my birthday, helped me get my G.E.D, and even went through the pain staking steps of getting me through the testing required to get into college.

Although I wasn't unguarded enough to really feel at home, I started to feel a calming sense of belonging. Unfortunately, in this new comfort, I became restless. Something felt missing from my life, it didn't feel right. I got a job at a boutique at our local mall and spent most of my days working, going to school, then spending my free time in my bedroom - working on crafts or reading. I've always had this deep urge inside of becoming a successful entrepreneur. I started off with modeling, acting, and belly dancing. I also started a custom pillow shop on Etsy to bring in some extra cash. The interest to become an actress took a more meaningful turn when I sat down and wrote a full movie script. I then took that script and tried finding actors to fill roles for the movie. I hosted meetings between my actors and film investors, determined to

THE EDGE OF BROKEN

convince someone my script would make a great film. This was all so exciting. I had the stability provided at my aunt and uncles, and nurtured my creative side to start a business of one kind or another.

As I felt I was making head way, my uncle and I began to butt heads. He wanted my focus to stay on my job and school until I graduated, so that I wouldn't get distracted with other stuff. Although I loved him and adored him for everything he had done to help me, I just couldn't agree. Something was tugging at me, making me long for something more than where I was. Still longing for this need to build something bigger than my life in that moment. I didn't want to just go to college, get some degree, and work a 9 to 5 for the rest of my life. What I had at my aunt and uncle's home was a comfort I had never known, and it didn't feel right to me, it didn't feel like I was moving forward. In fact, I almost felt like life was getting boring and stagnant. I didn't want the chaos I had always known, but I needed more inspiration to fulfill the dream I had brewing inside of me.

My uncle and I ended up getting into some strong disagreements that really put a wedge between our relationship. I decided it was time for me to start saving up money to move out on my own. I knew everything my new family was doing was to ensure I had a great life, but for some reason I felt like I was drowning all over again. I felt like I wasn't in the right place, wasn't achieving my dreams fast enough, and it was putting me into a panic that caused friction in my relationship with my uncle. I couldn't explain my emotions, I just knew they consumed me.

I knew what I was making at my job at the mall would never get me into an apartment, the market was too expensive. I started searching online for alternative income opportunities on Craigslist. That's when I found out about the adult industry, more specifically, web cam modelling. Now, the next few decisions I'd make in my life aren't a period I'm proud of, but I'm also not ashamed of it. It was a process I went through that I grew in my own way. It was the first unofficial "career" I'd build as an entrepreneur, and as dark and stigmatized as the adult industry is, and how against my deep core Christian beliefs it was, I saw the opportunity of income. Fueled by desperation to get my own place and start a new life - I jumped into web cam modelling.

As someone who's been through abuse, I knew I could never get into the porn industry, or anything that involved being touched by men. I struggled enough as it was to be kissed by someone I was attracted to, I had no intention of having intercourse with a complete stranger. I made a personal vow that I'd never cross that line, I don't think I physically would have been able to regardless. I propped up a webcam, recorded a few things, put them online, and made money per view and from donations from "fans." Before I knew it, I was quickly making good money. Great money. The kind of money I never thought could exist. It all felt surreal in the beginning. For only a few day's worth of work, my account now had a balance of a few thousand dollars. I figured there was no way I was getting that money, there had to be a catch. When I hit that deposit button and the cash actually posted in my bank account a few days later, I was in shock and awe. This would be my ticket to starting my own life, albeit not the best solution, it was the one available. I felt guilty for what I was doing, prayed to God a lot about my decisions that I was making, and although I should have never gotten into the industry to begin with, I promised Him that once I found something else that was sustainable, I would get out of it immediately.

After a month, I had more than enough money in my account to make my move. It was a tension-built transition into my own place, but I left my uncle's home amicably. I knew I was going to miss them, aside from my siblings, they had been the only true sense of family I had felt in a while. Leaving the stability of my new life was a bit worrisome, but I didn't feel like I was making the wrong decision. I knew I had to venture back out on my own. I had always been alone, and even in my struggles, I grew more and learned more through my independence. I struggled the most, mentally and emotionally, when I lived with other people. It was time to be alone again, that was how I thrived, or so I thought.

Being by myself did feel lonely but it was what I knew best. I moved into a two-bedroom apartment and focused half my time on the webcam work and the other half on my movie. I ended up falling for the lead act I had secured for the movie's role. Expectations of the "relationship" were not on steady ground and things turned upside down. My emotions got the best of me, and I threw the whole movie concept out the window, determined to forget about it forever. Feeling hurt and abandoned, I decided to fill my days working more hours in the adult industry.

Eventually, I was getting sick of the webcam work. I sat home all day alone and felt bored and frustrated. I researched other opportunities in the adult industry, being selective of what I would get into. First, I got into nude modeling. I ditched that pretty quickly after doing some shots at a man's house, only for him to stop mid-way to pleasure himself in front of me. I then tried working at a local strip club - that only lasted a couple of weeks after one of the strippers stole all of my tips from my purse. That night, I wasn't the best version of myself, I flipped tables over in anger for having all of my night's worth of work gone in seconds. The whole atmosphere in the club felt toxic and I knew I didn't belong in this setting. Most of the women were always drunk or high on heavy drugs.

It was only after I started working for a private strip company in Nashville, that I finally settled into a steady second role. We'd visit bachelor parties and the like, giving dances and serving food and alcohol in lingerie. Some nights were an absolute bore, others were glamorous. We spent days on luxurious yachts, beautiful mansions I'd never thought I'd step foot in, and surrounded by some high dollar figures. On the opposite end of that, I also found myself in some seedy places I'd never step back in again. We did events from frat boys, to biker gangs, and even celebrities.

It was in this line of work that I met my best friend, Barbie. Her nickname of course, but it suited her. Barbie and I were like night and day. She was the epitome of her name, and I was this tall scrawny brunette that didn't look at all like I belonged in the industry. But we became instant friends and spent nearly every day together, even when we weren't working. We both attended each other's shows to be the "back-up" in the event some drunk guys got a little rowdy. I adored her. She was the only true friend I had at that time in my life, and her happy spirit really kept me going, even on my darkest days.

Soon again, I would be distraught with boredom. Life became to consistent and comfortable. Was I working in the best industry in the world? No. But even in its own form of excitement, the daily routine was getting mundane and I was getting tired of the line of work I was in. Drunk guys don't make the best customers. I was getting frustrated. I got into this world to help fund my way into a new life, and now I felt like I was stuck, with no end in sight. I started making plans to leave, wanting to pursue my original goals of travelling the world. I bought a van for $1000, spent money on it to make it comfortable enough to live in, then moved out of my two-bedroom apartment complex. Still keeping my Honda, I moved into my van with my lab/pit mix Anoki.

I decided I'd get used to living in the van for a month or two as I saved up some money to finally pull the trigger of hitting the road. I wanted to road trip across the U.S. in hopes it would help me find a new life to start somewhere fresh. It didn't take too long before my idea of living out of a van went south. The space was cramped, to say in the least. I felt even more cramped and limited than when I was living in my tent. I was also surprised by how difficult it was to find parking space for my van every night. Couldn't park at the general places, like Walmart, because I felt way too exposed as a young 19-year-old girl to all of the semi-truck drivers. Every time I parked somewhere in an apartment complex, I'd get a "move your butt out of here" kind of ticket. Just about everywhere I was going, I was getting the boot.

A little over a month had passed and I wasn't having much luck finding a place to consistently park my van at night. This wasn't turning out to be how I had expected, and I still hadn't saved enough money for my trip across the U.S. I had steady income and I didn't want to leave it till I had netting to fall back on. Then, I made the wild decision to move into a storage unit. Yup, that's right, a storage unit. Homeless lifestyle? I've nearly lived them all. In a tent in the woods, out of my car, out of my van, and now in a storage unit. Now, if you're asking, do they even let you live in those things? The answer is a hard no. I had to "secretly" live in a storage unit, and before I'd know it, I'd be living in one for 4 months. I sold my van for a few hundred bucks, because it just wasn't doing the job, and used my Honda Civic to get around after I moved into my new "pad."

I worked mostly at night, so staying in the storage unit area wasn't super suspicious during the day. I did my best to keep myself busy, avoiding my unit as much as possible. I also worked late with my stripping job, so I tried pulling into my storage area around 4-5 in the morning, then sleeping till about noon. I'd park my car right in front of the unit, keep the door cracked open a few inches, then I'd crash out on a small black chair that folded open into a twin size bed.

I had a few neighboring storage unit guests that worked in their units with craft stuff, so it really helped me build a cover that I was in there working. I set up a small paint and writing station to use as a ploy if anyone ever confronted me. I don't know the rules about working in a storage unit complex in most places, but the owners of this place fortunately didn't seem to care. Similar to living out of my tent, I set up the décor in my storage unit to help me get the sense my living quarters were a little more than a mundane storage unit.

I decorated the walls with bookshelves I bought from Walmart and filled them with hundreds of books to keep me entertained. I also set up a small vanity area, bought a fuzzy pink rug, and made the place cozy and chic. Just like the tent days, I purchased a camping toilet for the at-home emergencies and purchased a large plastic tub to bathe in. The bucket was actually big enough for me to sit in, outstretched. I'd fill a few jugs with water I'd get from the park I took Anoki to for his daily walks. They had a public in-ground pump and I collected the water I needed to bathe. I had a decent set-up. I felt the freedom of not having bills, aside from the $150 I paid for the unit's monthly fee, which included the electricity. But, I couldn't live in a storage unit for as long as I did, without eventually getting caught. Most people couldn't even manage living in it for a couple of days without being noticed, but it was one of those rare strokes of luck that I went unnoticed for as long as I did.

One morning, I was startled awake to the loud sound of my storage door being thrown open. If you've ever rented from a storage unit, you know the garage doors make a loud rattling sound on their way up. I shot up from an exhausted sleep, my heart pounding. I tried to see through tired eyes, wiping them desperately to catch a glimpse of what was going on through the bright afternoon light pouring in. When I could finally see my surroundings well enough, I noticed a man in his late 60's glaring down at me. I covered myself to my shoulders with my blanket, a chill running up my spine for getting caught. Then his face softened. It must have been the fear in my eyes that changed the pace of his mood, but instead of yelling, he asked calmly what I was doing.

I was a young 19-year-old girl sleeping in a storage unit, it obviously dawned on him that I didn't have a home, and I was grateful for his patient questioning. He had grown suspicious of my unit when he started noticing the numerous evening clock-ins they saw in their log. He had assumed that I must have been caught up in some sort of drug or prostitution ordeal. I explained that I was living out of my car, trying to save up to move into a new home, adding that I was staying temporarily in the storage unit because it was the only safe place I could find. He was a compassionate soul. Since I wasn't causing any trouble, he told me it was alright that I stayed for a little while longer, but that I had to promise to do my best not to let others notice. I was incredibly grateful for his kindness. This strange man had all the right in the world to kick me off his business's property, yet he allowed me to stay, and for that, I was incredibly blessed.

During my stay in the unit, I went through a variety of relationships. I had set up an account on an online dating site and most of the men I met went no further than the first date. When I started getting tired of the whole dating scene, I made the decision to remove my online dating profile. When I logged in to delete it, I saw that I had an unread message from someone new. I glanced over his profile and became a little intrigued. He was attractive and seemed normal, his message to me a polite introduction and hello.

"Here is my number, I'm deleting my account today, you can text me if you want." I messaged back to his hello, then I deleted the account.

It wasn't long before he sent a text and we were spending hours every day getting to know one another. He asked me out on an official first date, and although I had every inclination not to show up because I wasn't feeling well, I felt the urge to go. I was instantly attracted to him, and we had a wonderful time over dinner getting to know one another. We spent the rest of the night sneaking through a closed park. It felt incredibly romantic and our chemistry just clicked. The more we talked, the more we realized how similar our tastes were, and for the first time in a long time, I really enjoyed my date.

Things between Cameron and I moved quickly. After our first night together, we found ourselves immediately drawn to each other. Now spending nearly every day together, we met between our work and his school schedule. I kept the real industry I was in a secret and told him I worked odd hours because I was in acting and modeling. Didn't find much of an urge to tell him I was living out of a storage unit, either. I was sure that would scare him off and I was enjoying his company too much to let him see how crazy my situation was.

Eventually, I couldn't hide where I was living any longer. He was inquisitive about where I lived and wanted to spend some time at my place, instead of his parent's place all the time. He was living with them while finishing off trade school. So, nervously, I brought him to my spectacular pad, then waited for him to take off running. To my surprise, Cameron was fascinated with my life in a storage unit. Our relationship quickly blossomed. One evening, after an intense fight with his parents, he ended up packing his stuff and moved in with me. Now we were storage unit roommates.

Within 3 days of meeting him, he had claimed our relationship exclusive, within a month he told me he loved me. Unlike the relationships that came before him, I was comfortable with Cameron. We had great chemistry which solidified our romantic connection. In the past, I struggled even kissing guys without being drawn back into memories of my abuse. If I ended up sleeping with a boyfriend, I was generally the one to wake up in the middle of the night and sneak off before they woke up, going home feeling nauseated. I associated all of this to my sexual abuse. Anytime I became intimate with a guy, the memories would be intense. I'd feel sick to my stomach and always had to get away from their touch. It made me feel guilty, but my actions were so strongly based on my emotions, emotions I had a hard time controlling when it came to my past.

Cameron was different. When I kissed him, my belly didn't hurt. The awful memories didn't come rushing through my mind. I enjoyed the moments with him, not thinking about everything that had hurt me before. This was a brand-new experience and I knew it meant something. The first day we became intimate, I wanted to lay in his arms forever. I felt safe with him, I felt happy with him, I felt normal with him. Even through this puppy-love faze, I always noticed that somedays he would act off, vulgar even. He'd turn into someone so different from the guy I was with the day before, that I was starting to become wary and irritated with him.

It was a couple of months into our relationship, a couple of weeks after he had moved in with me, that I found out I had fallen in love with a drug addict. He struggled with years of substance abuse. Around the same time I found out about his addiction, I also found out that I was pregnant. Living out of a storage unit, unmarried, in a relationship that was about to be bashed against the rocks, and I had a baby on the way.

Just as I started thinking, there is no way life can get worse, you throw this loop in, God. Good one, you have a serious sense of humor, I thought. I had faith in that things in life happened for certain reasons, so I figured if He put this on my shoulders, I must have the solution to get through it. Now I had to figure out what the heck that solution was.

5.

FIGHTING DEPRESSION

Cameron and I's relationship began to unravel long before we had any real time to bond. Throw a baby into the mix and all hell broke loose. Cameron loved me, that was never a question. He was both excited about the baby and nervous because of our living conditions, or lack of. I was in a full blown panic because we weren't prepared and Cameron's drug addiction was severe. I had no experience with drug addiction first hand and had a hard time empathizing with the situation. I had never so much as drank or smoke in my life, and hardened by my past, I couldn't come to terms with his battle. I didn't understand what addiction meant, then. I took the addiction personally, and when it turned into lying and sneaking around, it really made me pull away. I hardened against Cameron, lost in a mixture of emotions towards him. I was excited for the baby, I knew from an early age that I'd be a young mother when I met the right guy. I just never thought it would happened when I was 19-years-old and homeless in a storage unit. Cameron was working part time at a local golf course, only making $9/hour and I was still caught up in the adult industry. If I quit work because of the pregnancy, Cameron wouldn't have enough coming into to take care of us. He was in school full time for welding and was only a short time away from graduating, so we made the decision that I would continue to work until we had enough saved, and until he graduated and landed a well-paying job. After he secured a new position, I planned to fully transition out of the work I was doing.

It was a few months into our relationship before I disclosed to Cameron what I was really doing. He was understandably furious about it all. He wasn't the one to demand I ever quit anything, but his temper showed his disapproval. I knew he was upset, but we talked about the money it was bringing and knew it was needed now that we were expecting. He became incredibly protective and accompanied me on most events when he wasn't in classes. We had finally had enough saved aside for us to move into a small one-bedroom apartment. It was about

$500/month and located in probably one of the worst areas and neighborhoods you could find around Nashville. Since beggars couldn't be choosers, we made do with what we could afford. Obviously raising a child in a storage unit is out of the question.

We packed up what little we had and moved in to our new place. Cam and I's already fragile relationship led to tense fights, coupled with all the upcoming stresses of a new baby. I'd get so angry and react so violently, I hardly recognized myself. An accumulation of money problems, the stress of pregnancy and not being prepared, and the process of Cameron fighting his drug addiction led to an unhealthy emotional atmosphere. We hadn't had enough time to really learn anything about each other, not on a deeper level. Here we were, trying to figure ourselves out and learning how to love each other, at a time in our lives where we were both at our lowest points. We had a lot of work to do and we had to do it fast. We'd be introducing a new baby girl into the world in a few months.

My pregnancy with Noelle was difficult. I couldn't get off the couch without running to the bathroom to throw up every single time. I felt and looked like death. I couldn't keep anything down, including water. I was hospitalized multiple times through the pregnancy just to get some fluids into my system. I was religiously on Zofran, but it couldn't fully cut through the severity of my nausea. I didn't get blessed with having a comfortable and happy pregnancy, and there wasn't a thing about me that glowed. I was falling apart. Physically and emotionally. It meant I couldn't work which meant less money was coming in. This was nerve racking, but a pregnant mother should never work in the adult industry, so it was a blessing in disguise. A really difficult disguise. When Cameron finally graduated, he landed a well-paying position at a local fabrication shop for his welding skills. Although it wasn't a high paying position, it was enough for me to put the adult industry to bed and focus on getting through my pregnancy, so we could have a healthy baby girl. We still had a long way to go before we could afford to get out of the apartment complex we were living in. It seemed to be on the news at least once a month for a shooting. Nothing says great living conditions like being barricaded in your apartment complex while the FBI and SWAT tear through the neighboring buildings, looking for a criminal.

Living there was nothing short of being miserable. I found more peace living in a tent than living in this small dirty apartment. To make matters worse, it had a severe cockroach infestation. We had the place sprayed so many times, but it never mattered. They had to be living in every crevice of every single wall in that building, it was horrendous. You'd get up to get a glass of water in the middle of the night, switch the light on, and watch disgusted as the roaches ran across all the walls to hide behind a dark corner. I never knew how much of a pest German Cockroaches were until they infested every part of our home.

I was bringing my daughter into this world, a child I had always imagined and told myself would never live through the poverty and depression I had grown up in, but that is exactly what she was being born into. I was defeated. I cried myself to sleep nearly every night. While Cameron slept, I spent countless nights in the bathroom, trying not to wake him through the tears and sobbing. Sick, unattached in my relationship, and living in what was only a step above what felt like trash, I just couldn't believe how often I felt crapped on by the universe. I knew the pregnancy was through our own choices, but we certainly didn't expect a baby out of one careless night. I wasn't upset about my misfortune, I was angry that I'd be bringing a child into it.

Being homeless when I was on my own wasn't difficult to get through. I was a minimalist, I didn't need much. I could live with the bare minimum, pack my bags, and travel the world. Now I had a baby to look after, it was no longer simple. I didn't have the freedom to do what I wanted, live where I wanted, or go where I wanted. I needed to start building some roots fast, so I could bring my daughter into a somewhat stable world, and even more important, stable parents. We did everything we could to get the home cleaned up and furnished in time for our little love to join us. Most of the stuff we received were hand me downs, but I was picky about what I would put my daughter in. Call it foolish pride, even though we were poor, I'd splurge any opportunity we had on Noelle.

Both Cameron and I's parents were a God-send through the pregnancy. Even though my relationship with my parents still was strained, going through the pregnancy really brought us a lot closer together. They helped by sending money and buying necessities for Noelle. Our little girl decided to join the world on July 22nd of 2013, at 37 weeks, and weighing in at a tiny 6 pounds. Although I was nervous about the whole process, labor was a breeze. It was what came after labor that I wasn't prepared for. Days of wearing pads that belonged to giants, or diaper pads that didn't do much to compliment an already flat backside. No one ever talked about the squirt bottle I'd be using to clean with after using the restroom, no one talked about the pain when your nurse came into the room to push on your sore belly to ensure you didn't clot. There was a lot in the post-pregnancy stage I never was prepared for and I was a hot mess.

My parents had decided to come up to Nashville to meet Cameron and his family and be supportive through the last few weeks of my pregnancy. It was a wonderful surprise for them that Noelle came two days before they were set to leave. They had the opportunity to meet her in the hospital and be a part of the experience. The first time Cameron held Noelle in his arms, he was in tears. Looking at him then and there, holding our precious daughter, so caught up in his emotions of love, I knew we'd make it. I knew the road ahead of us would be long and exhausting, but if we held on, our love would get us through it. Regardless of the struggles he was personally facing, he was a wonderful man and would prove to be an even better husband and father. Watching his patience and love with Noelle was such a refreshing change to the atmosphere I had grown up in as a child that it filled me to the brim with love. I knew we were poor, and at that point in our lives, we didn't have much to offer. However, Noelle had two parents that loved her beyond words and she would blossom in that love. She was a healthy and beautiful little baby girl with a thick head of dark brown hair and warm brown eyes.

Despite the love and happiness that came with having our daughter, it didn't change my emotional make up. Even in the beautiful parts of life, the times when your heart is full to the top with love for the people around you, depression can still be the closest friend you have. The friend that doesn't know how to leave, the one you don't know how to push away. I loved my family, but I hated myself. Although raising a newborn is just as hard as any job, especially since Noelle was a difficult baby, I didn't have the type of job that really took me away from my thoughts. Because of that, the depression thundered in. I was sitting at home all day long with an angry newborn, sleep deprived and still unhealthy from how hard the pregnancy had affected me. I was the perfect victim. I had spent a lifetime pushing the weight of depression away, to now have it swing around and hit me full force in my solitude. I always seemed to struggle the most when life seemed to be heading in a good direction. A self-sabotage of sorts. Even though life wasn't perfect, it was slowly getting better, and it was during those times I suffered the most.

Anxiety wrapped itself around me, consuming me with thoughts of "what ifs." What if Noelle died, what if she got cancer, what if Cameron lost his job, and so on. Through that anxiety came the depression. Through the depression came the anger. Through that anger, I'd find ways to self-sabotage my life. The more life seemed steady, surrounded by love, the more I was reminded that I was a stranger to this world and didn't fit in. I was reminded that the world said I didn't deserve happiness and fully believed this part of my life was a delusion. A way to trick me into happiness, only to wipe it out from under me and break me completely.

Depression is a difficult thing to explain. There are thousands of medical articles on Google that do their best to explain what it is, but they always fall short. For me, depression always felt like that last breath before dying. Everything hurts, you don't want to go, but at this point, you just want to escape the pain. You know you'll miss the people you love, but your mind is so foggy and your whole body and soul in agony, that dying feels like the better choice. Depression feels like you're stuck in that moment for years. I just wanted to die because it hurt, but I ached for the people I'd leave behind. With this depression came the urge to commit suicide. For years I was tempted by the idea that taking my life would be the best decision. Not only would I no longer have to suffer, the people around me would no longer have to suffer by putting up with me. I held a knife to my wrist countless times, willing myself to cut, but unable to find the courage to go through with it. Which would bring its own onslaught of emotional abuse, I'd think I was an absolute coward.

My depression hurt my relationship with Cameron, terribly. I didn't trust him. I lived in this delusional state that he thought I was worthless, consumed by my own insecurities. I always felt like I wasn't good enough. Wasn't beautiful enough. Wasn't smart enough. I never felt good about myself and I let my anger from my sadness consume me. The moment I saw a pretty girl in a room with us, the moment I saw someone beautiful on

T.V., I'd snap on Cameron for thinking she was better than me. Of course, he'd sit there, mouth gaping, wondering what in the world was I thinking – but I reflected all of my internal emotions onto him. He became my punching bag for my pain.

Depression isn't just sadness. It isn't just sitting there crying and moping every day. Sure, that's part of it, but there are so many layers to depression. It comes in furious anger, it comes in crying till your lungs burn, and it comes in absolute silence. The anger and the sadness are an outward portrayal of your fight with depression. The silence, that one is the hardest to get through. That's your inner turmoil in all its absolute darkness, seen by no one, suffered alone. Even when you get past the crying and yelling, the silence can live in us for the rest of our lives. It keeps us from getting out of bed and from feeling alive, it puts us in a zombie-like trance and keeps us glued to this condition. It feels inescapable and like death itself.

There aren't enough articles on Google to really take in the capacity of depression in its entirety. Unless one has experienced it firsthand, it really can't be put into words. I know it's a mental struggle, but it feels so strong, that most days the pain feels physical. It's suffocating. Your body feels numb and achy, and it hurts to get up and do anything. It's this thick black goop inside of you that is filled with your absolute worst traits, and no matter how much you pull and pull and pull, the more you struggle against it, the deeper it drags you in.

When I was staying with my grandparents, they had me visit a psychologist to discuss my issues. I gave her the jist of everything I had been through and she prescribed me anti-depressants. Those pills didn't do a thing aside from putting me in a sleep trance. I was irritated by what I felt was a lazy approach to addressing my problems. I wasn't depressed because I had some chemical imbalance in my head. Although that is its own crippling form of depression, it wasn't what I had. That is the problem with depression. Nobody truly understands the varying levels and remedies to help fix it. Someone else's pill wasn't my cure. I was depressed because I had gone through horrific abuse my whole life growing up, I ran away to find an escape and felt betrayed by everyone in the world I thought was meant to love me, and she thought some pill would do the trick to "fix" me. I still feel angry about that to this day. There is a stigma around it that makes doctors and psychologists assume a simple pill will fix everyone. I just wanted to learn how to escape my own head and the pain that had built up in there – not live in a fog the rest of my life.

I've heard some people say that they would rather live through a zombie-like state than deal with the depressing thoughts, but not me. I'd rather deal with them and face them head on than be out-of-touch with the world while it sped past me. I didn't *want* to be depressed, so I didn't want some pill to mask my problem. I wanted to live, I wanted to know happiness, I wanted to face it so I could learn to conquer it. I knew it would be hard, but I chose to go through it as it was. I refused to take medicine to fog my mind from it. My past wasn't chemical, it was physical and real, and I just needed to know how to heal on the same level.

My pain wouldn't go away with medicine. It would live with me through every touch, every close breath, and everyone who stood an inch too close to me. It would always be there, and if I didn't take it head on, it would never go away. Depression is hard, but one of the hardest parts of it is not knowing a life without depression. I had never had a moment in my life where I was happy, and I mean truly happy. Even on the days I felt my best, it always lingered in the background like a black shadow. I had always known some level of depression throughout my life and depending on the condition of where I was at that moment in time, it went from mild to violent. I didn't know how to be happy, so I didn't know where to look for it or how to find it. Mix that with conditions of starting a new family in a rough living environment, and I felt like I'd never became familiar to this elusive happiness.

On top of the depression and suicidal tendencies, I had horrific anxiety. I still, to this day, try to learn how to manage my panic attacks. When I first used to have them, I thought I was having a heart attack. I couldn't breathe, couldn't catch a full breath, I felt like I needed to rip out of my skin and crawl out of my body. Living in a state of mind where you are a mental wreck, at all times, is exhausting.

I learned to hold onto life for my daughter and my husband. Did I want to kill myself? Yes often, to get away from the endless pain. But, I refused. I would never take my life and I would fight through the mental breakdowns. No one would be there to raise and protect my daughter in my place. I didn't trust the world or anyone in it. Even with how much of a loving father Cameron was, he didn't have the life experiences I had. He wasn't fully aware of the threats society can have on young innocent little girls.

Although the sadness lived in every part of my soul, I had just enough of a spark to give me the will to fight. I knew, one day, I fight away from the haunting darkness. One day, I promised myself, the molestations wouldn't repeat over and over in my head. One day, I'd stop feeling like I was a failure and worthless. To change my life, I just had to keep taking a few steps forward, and I knew those steps would eventually add up.

I had to make a change, I knew that. If I was committed to producing a life for my child that I had always vowed I would give her - I'd have to put the depression to the back burner and start building the life that I wanted for myself and my family. I couldn't let the depression consume me to the point I was playing the victim everyday of my life. I wanted amazing things, and I couldn't achieve that if I sat idly by and let the emotions I felt take control. I refused. *I* was going to take control of *it*. I had spent my whole life a victim to other people's bad decisions. Now, it was my turn to make decisions that outlined my future, and I wasn't going to make the same mistakes others had.

I was investing too much of my thoughts and time into a period of my life that I had no control over. Moping about things in the past, and the "what ifs," led nowhere. I had control now, I just needed to figure out how to take charge of my own life and emotions. It no longer made sense to continue letting my life be ruined emotionally, because of my scarring past. I had a hard start, but I was now free from the chains that bound me as a child to my abusers. I wanted a beautiful house, I wanted my family to have security, I wanted to travel the world and experience all of its beauty and escape from this darkness that I had known forever.

I wasn't going to play the victim, I wasn't going to sit around and think about all the things I had gone through and feel sorry for myself. How would that benefit me? It wouldn't. It wouldn't benefit raising my daughter, either. In fact, choosing to stay a victim to my past meant I stayed a victim to the people who abused me, and like hell would I give them any more power at this point in my life. Power over me meant power over the way my daughter was raised, and I wouldn't let them touch her.

I didn't know where to begin but I knew I had to do something. We only had one working vehicle at the time, which Cameron used for work. Since I refused to put Noelle into any form of daycare, especially in the area we were living in, I had to come up with the perfect plan to make money from home. It was time to put my creative cap on and figure out a solution to do just that. I pulled out an old beat-up laptop and started looking up ways to make money online. Now, if you have ever done this, you may be familiar with the thousands of methods that are available. You'd also probably know that 999 of that thousand is an absolute waste of time, and sometimes even money. I couldn't afford to buy anything to sell, so I looked up "free" ways to make money.

Regardless, I was excited to take on this challenge. I've always been a competitive person, so this was a unique approach to conquer something new. I was dedicated to finding some type of job to take on from the comfort of home that would produce a second steady stream of income. I wanted to make money while still getting the benefit of being a stay at home mom. My new entrepreneurial journey had begun.

6.

FACING ENTREPRENEURSHIP

I can't tell you the number of things I got pulled into, trying to figure out how to make money online. I mean, some of the things I did, like getting paid 10 cents to watch 5-minute videos, screamed desperation. I wasn't even getting paid minimum wage! At that rate, I was lucky if I made $1.50 every hour. Ridiculous to think about now, but I wanted to learn something that provided an opportunity to bring in an income. I wanted to learn something, anything, that would help me provide financial security for our family. It wouldn't take too long to realize the online gimmicks were a joke. I put so much energy into programs that didn't produce anything more than a few cents. Wasted time, but I took the positive, and chalked it up to gaining experience.

Although I was aware of social media platforms like Facebook, Instagram, and Pinterest I wasn't active on them. I only had a Facebook account and rarely posted on it. In fact, when I did start actively using social media, I had to go through and "clean house" of all the posts that I made through my early teens, which didn't present a professional atmosphere. I eventually stumbled across Pinterest in my search for an online career and really became intrigued with the fashion industry. After a year of working ridiculous gigs online to make pennies on the dollar, I started forming an idea to build a real company that sold real products, instead of taking dumb quizzes online for a quarter.

It was then I decided I'd open an online boutique. The tricky part was figuring out how to sell products without the money to purchase them in the first place. When I stayed with my aunt and uncle, I had an Etsy shop selling custom pillows, so jumped back on the Etsy industry to sell custom dresses. Not the right side of the industry I wanted to get into, but I had some experience from my days in high school in an elective class on how to sew clothes, so that's where I started. I'd find pictures of dresses online I was confident I could make at a lower rate and would list them on my Etsy shop. Since Etsy is all about promoting hand-made custom goods, it was the right platform for me. I could wait till I had a sale come through, use the money to purchase the product to make the dress, then ship it to my customers.

Etsy and JoAnn's became my best friends. Surprisingly, it didn't take long to make decent money. I was nowhere on my way to making riches, but I was making enough to pay a few bills. It eventually became frustrating that there was only so much I could take on in a month and not really grow from there. I wasn't making enough money to hire someone else to help scale the business, I barely had enough profit to cover my own utilities. It was time to move in a new direction. I researched what I had wanted to do in the first place, which was purchasing boutique clothing at wholesale to sell on my own website.

I stumbled across a beautiful drop-ship company that allowed me to list their products on my website, then sell them and take a commission from that sale. Meaning, I didn't have to carry any stock. They did all the shipping, put my branding on the box and receipts, and would send the product to my customers. I went from making a couple hundred bucks in profit every month to then jumping into making about $1,500 a month. Again, nothing phenomenal, but I was pulling in more than Cameron was – and that was insane when you compared the effort he put into his career. I woke up every morning, got Noelle situated, made myself a cup of tea, and went to work on my computer.

Having my online boutique really taught me a lot about building a strong brand and learning how to use social media to generate business. Because I couldn't afford to hire a graphic designer or web builder, I watched 1000's of videos on web design and graphic design. To my surprise, I had an eye for it. Even though my website and company were brand new, the quality of the site and the designs became appealing to customers and started pulling in a good chunk of change every month. It still wasn't enough, though. With each commission on a $60 dress, I was making about $5. I knew if I could purchase my own wholesale products, I could get a bigger cut for the same exact product. I refocused and started saving money to invest into my own wholesale merchandise.

This was such an exciting experience. Broke as dirt, I somehow, after working and studying techniques online for nearly a year, stumbled on something that allowed me to work a real job from home. I was pulling in a few thousand dollars every month to help sustain our family. We still lived paycheck to paycheck because of our enormous debt, but we were slowly able to grow our savings. It never really accumulated over much since I reinvested most of my income back into the business, but we had just enough to fall back on for emergencies.

Before I knew it, our tiny 1-bedroom apartment was lined with layers of racks holding the clothes I had purchased for the company. Business was doing well, and I felt an incredible sense of accomplishment. For as long as I could remember, I've been a worker. My mind and hands always had to be busy working on something that led to opportunity in the future.

Although I didn't thrive working for other people and companies, I loved being in business for myself. Having my own company really gave me a sense of pride that inspired me to work harder and grow bigger.

I was still living in the same crappy apartment, still lugging laundry at midnight to the laundry mat three buildings away, and still fighting an overwhelming amount of depression and anxiety. But, for the first time in a long time, I saw a slight glimmer of light at the end of the tunnel. I knew I was going to work on my business for a long time before it made a break and brought in income that really stabilized us, but I saw the light, and I knew if I kept going, I'd eventually get there.

About a year after Noelle's birth, Cameron and I were expecting again. During that time, we had made plans to get married in Gatlinburg. It was a small event with Cameron and I's parents and siblings. The wedding day was incredibly rough. This pregnancy was a lot harder than it was with Noelle. I knew my first experience with

Noelle was rough, but there was something about this one that my gut said was really wrong. I was sick the night of my wedding, I threw up all the way till I was in front of the preacher saying, "I do." I had enough distractions through the ceremony to keep from vomiting, but I couldn't stand on my feet for long. The nausea was overpowering. My parents treated us to dinner at a beautiful steakhouse after the ceremony, and white dress and all, I couldn't take a single bite, sitting at the table with a trash can in my lap and my head in it all throughout the night.

The wedding was beautiful and intimate, but I didn't get to enjoy much of it from how terrible I was feeling. When we got back home, things progressively worsened. No matter how many times we went to the hospital, the doctors would put me on I.V. fluids, give me nausea medication that kept my head out of the toilet for a few hours, and would send me home telling me everything was alright. My concern and intuition that something was strange about this pregnancy was made real when I woke up one night to see my pants soaked in blood.

We rushed Noelle over to Cameron's parent's house, then made our way to the E.R. The whole drive there, I cried. I knew we had lost the baby. I could just tell. There was something wrong, and I knew there was no way that this baby was going to make it. To my surprise and irritation, the nurses at the women's hospital told me everything was fine, the baby had a heartbeat, and nothing was abnormal. I was to just "keep an eye" on the bleeding. I was furious. Call it intuition, call it what you will, but I knew there wasn't a thing that was "alright" about this pregnancy. This may have only been my second one, but I had already experienced sickness with Noelle, and knew there was something strange going on this time around.

A few days later, I started having an odd sharp pain in my head. I'd been prone to a few migraines here and there, but never something like this. It was like the tip of a knife was poking the back of my head in only one spot. The pain was unbearable and wouldn't move from that one area. It didn't vibrate throughout the rest of my head or my neck like most of my migraines did. It was odd, but I took a migraine pill and went to bed, hoping that by the morning, it would be gone. I woke up early that morning, screaming in absolute agony. It felt like my left arm was rolling into itself, almost as if my bones were breaking. I screamed for Cameron's name to help, the pain was nothing like I had ever felt in my life, and just as his name passed my lips, I passed out.

I woke up in the bathroom, I had somehow stumbled my way in there with no recollection of doing so. I was soaked in my own pee, nauseous, and disoriented. Cameron was standing by my side, asking if I was okay.

He was just as confused and disoriented by what had occurred.

"I think you had a seizure," he said.

I had never had a seizure in my life prior to this incident, so I had no idea what it was like to go through one.

"I need you to call an ambulance," I told him.

"Can you get up and walk, I'll drive you to the hospital. You know how expensive the ambulance is going to be, we won't have the money for it."

I tried standing up and instantly collapsed to the floor. We lived on the second story of our apartment complex, there would be no way I was making my way down those stairs.

"No!" I yelled at him. "Cameron, there is seriously something wrong, you need to call an ambulance *now*, I can't even get up, let alone walk down our stairs!"

I was starting to panic. He tried calming me down as he called 911. I don't remember how much time had passed while I lied on the floor, waiting. I didn't feel like myself, going in and out of sleepy haze. Time did seem to go by quickly, and before I knew it, I was lying down on a stretcher as the ambulance made its way to the emergency room. Cameron rushed to his parent's house to drop Noelle off, then would head over to meet me at the hospital. As I was pushed through the emergency entry, a few nurses walked up and started talking to the men who had attended me in the ambulance. I told them about the pain in my arm and how it felt like my bones were breaking, having a hard time explaining how it seemed to curl in on itself. All of a sudden, I started to feel the pain again. I screamed in agony. "It's happening again," I yelled to the nurses. My back lunged upwards off the bed as I tried to hold my arm straight, then a tingly sensation shot up my spine. Before I had another thought, the world went black.

I woke up a few hours later. The doctor had performed an emergency abortion. I had eclampsia at a stage in my pregnancy the doctor said he had never seen or heard of. The baby was dying, and in the process, it was killing me. They had to remove his precious body, so I had a chance of living, because the baby wouldn't live either way. I was heartbroken. To have lost a child in pregnancy, and in a way that was so traumatizing, did nothing to help my depression. I was not in a good place. I was happy to be alive, happy to be with my husband and with my daughter, but heartbroken that I had lost a child. The anger didn't take too long to kick in. The nurses and doctors I had pleaded with to do further examinations, when I would go to the E.R., always pushed me away and told me I was fine. If they had just listened, they could have found a way to save my baby and me from that awful night. They didn't listen, no one listened. I had to nearly lose my life, and lost the life of my son, before someone was finally convinced that there was something wrong.

It took a while to come out of the ugly place I ran to in my head. Weeks had gone by before I realized I had been so caught up in my anger and hurt, that I never asked my doctor what they had done with my child. "How could I have not thought of that," I yelled to myself. *I should have brought my baby home in an urn and made a place for him.* We had planned to name him Noah, even though the doctors never told us his gender, I knew in the way only a mother knows that he was going to be a boy. I hated myself. I had been so consumed by my emotions that I didn't think to ask about my baby boy and what had happened to his body. Furious I hadn't brought him home to put his ashes in an urn. Broken, thinking I was an absolute failure as a mother. *How could I have been so selfish not to have thought of bringing him home.*

On my next check-up, I asked my doctor what had happened to my child. "He was incinerated," he said. Yes, you read that correctly. I had just lost my baby in a traumatic way, and my doctors response to that was that he was sent off to be incinerated. The second those words passed his lips, I burst into tears. He tried apologizing, consoling me that what had happened was not my fault, but it was too late. I felt a morbid disgust towards him and my heart was shattered. I couldn't get out of the hospital gown fast enough. I spent an hour sitting in my car crying before I drove home.

His awful words still haunt me today, and although I've healed from the pain, I've never forgotten. I'll hold Noah near and dear to my heart, even if I didn't get to see his beautiful face in person, I know he was my baby and I'd think of him forever. The next few months went by as a blur. I drowned myself in my boutique business and kept busy in raising Noelle, doing what I could to push away the pain from losing a child. I always told myself that if I had lost him after I had given birth to him, I'd still be a broken woman.

I couldn't ever imagine the heartbreak of a parent losing their child after they built a bond with them when they arrived into the world. It made me sick to think about losing Noelle and I was so grateful to have my baby girl to hold onto. I did everything I could to move on emotionally and refocus on building a better life for Noelle. I couldn't let my pain consume me, I still had a beautiful and feisty little girl to raise, and even on the days she couldn't stand me, I loved her with all my heart.

Eventually, we'd start outgrowing our apartment. We wanted to find a home we could live in without the fear of being broken into every day. Even some of our neighbors were an absolute terror to live next to. Cameron had earned a few raises for his great work ethic and I was still pulling in a steady income, so we decided it was time to upgrade our living space. After a few months of searching, we finally found a beautiful 2-bedroom apartment in a gated community, and it was within our budget.

Noelle was ecstatic to finally have her own bedroom, and Cameron and I were happy to have some privacy. Even more happy that we now had a dedicated room for all of Noelle's toys, instead of on our bedroom floor. We started getting into a new rhythm and settled in comfortably. Keeping my thoughts busy with work always felt like an escape, so I focused on learning new marketing techniques to use online. Although I was using Facebook, it wasn't through paid ads, I was too nervous to invest any money into it since I didn't feel like we had enough coming in. Because of that, my growth was slow. We grew through word of mouth and ensuring customer experience was amazing, so they were encouraged to come back and shop with us again.

Life was starting to become steady again. I still lived in my depression, I still fought with Cameron like he was the worst thing that had happened to me in my life (he wasn't, it was my anger and depression talking), and I still felt like a failure to my daughter. Sure, we had upgraded our living condition, but it still wasn't anything I felt overly proud of. I wanted out of the apartment and into a home. A real home with a real backyard I could put a playground on and take Noelle out to play with it. A real home I could decorate and paint as I wished, especially during the holidays. I had to accept that we had made a move up, and I knew in time, bigger and better things would come if I just kept working hard. That was my motivation to get through the darkest days. We'd made a few progressive steps, we just needed to keep making a few more. I knew eventually we would be able to buy a home.

Not long after, I received an unexpected text message from my aunt who I had stayed with during my initial trip up to Nashville. She worked at a Keller Williams office and thought I'd be a great fit as a real estate agent, after seeing the promotional work I was doing online for my boutique. She took me out to lunch and told me that if I worked hard, she would pay my way into real estate. Getting a license is expensive and we just didn't have the money to spend on classes, testing, and licensing. Having her help unlocked doors I never would have been able to afford to on my own.

I knew, through seeing her career, the amount of potential the industry held. I started researching everything there was about real estate, joined tons of Facebook groups to learn more about the business, and studied like crazy to pass my classes and prepare for the quiz. The first time I took it, I failed the national exam.

Heartbroken, I went back to studying the books, and finally passed the second time.

It was disappointing to find out how long you had to wait, after your testing, to finally became active and able to work. I spent every day watching the State's website, refreshing it every morning in hopes that that day would be the day I could finally start making money as an agent. I was the most impatient person in the world and was itching to work and start making money in this lucrative business. I found out one sale could make me what a few months of selling boutique dresses did. That potential motivated me to give it my all.

When my license finally went active, I put aside all of the work I had done for the boutique and went head first into real estate. With the help of my cousin Kalista, who taught me everything I needed to survive on my own, I finally landed a client less than a month into my licensing. I closed on my first client's home 30 days after they found the perfect house. That closing produced a paycheck a little over $4,000 and I was ecstatic. I had never seen a check that big in my life with my name on it, and this was from *one* client. I closed the boutique and decided I would focus on real estate 100%. I sold everything at a heavily discounted rate to put towards buying things I needed for my new business.

Out of the blue, because we hadn't learned the first two times how the body works, Cameron and I were expecting again. That announcement was a little tough to swallow. As expected, I went through the whole getting sick-like-I-was-dying phase again. I was too sick to even get my head off the couch, let alone work and meet up with clients. I also lived with the fear of going through the same episode as my last pregnancy and was put into high risk pregnancy care. The unexpectedness of the pregnancy was devastating, I knew it would put a stop to my real estate pursuits for a while. A sticky situation since I had closed the online boutique and real estate required a real hands on role. The paycheck I had received from my closing started to slowly get eaten away by bills and I was falling behind on real estate dues.

Bedridden, I spent almost every day of the first trimester unable to get off the couch. Taking care of Noelle drained every bit of energy I could muster up. I'd run to the bathroom to throw up at least twice every time I got up to make her something to eat. I had fallen off the planet, and understandably, my aunt was a little frustrated with my disappearance. After talking to her about the pregnancy, letting her know that my one and only real estate check had gone to bills and debt, she was wonderful and covered a few hundred dollars of required payments. I was so afraid to spend a penny into anymore real estate stuff, that I thought there would be no way to keep the lights on next month. For her to have stepped in like she did was a testament to her giving heart.

Being poor is a hard state to be in. Even desperation and determination sometimes needs a little more help to get you over that edge. We were dirt poor and in massive debt, putting the real estate business to the side really hurt us financially. As soon as the sickness subsided during the second half of my second trimester, I dived right back into working. I even worked through labor, handling email communications as I laid on the bed waiting for my cervix to dilate. We had two little girls to look after now, there was no room for taking it easy.

Lylah was our blue-eyed little angel. She was pale, with light hair, and blue eyes that were the color of the sky. Cameron and I teased that she was the milkman's baby, we had no idea where she got her complexion and her eye color. A stranger could look at Noelle and tell she was ours. With her warm chocolate eyes and thick brown hair, and a spirit that matched my own, there was no denying she was our daughter. Lylah, on the other hand, was a calm sweet little baby and I joked for months that the hospital staff must have had her mixed up. She was a blessing, though. Her calm sweet nature made getting work done a lot easier. Between a 2-year-old and a newborn, and Cameron's fulltime work schedule, I had to make magic happen to build a successful real estate business.

Cameron and I went through two more early miscarriages, that left our hearts broken, and we finally decided that two kids would be more than enough for our family. Losing children was not only eating away at my mental health, but the pregnancies also broke down my physical health. I had now lost three babies, I couldn't go through this ever again. Noelle and Lylah would fill my heart and home and they would be all I needed. Like always, I escaped into my work to get away from the depression, putting 100% focus into raising my daughters and becoming a successful agent.

7.

BUILDING A REAL ESTATE CAREER

I became obsessive about real estate. I focused heavily on building a brand and presence that made me look established. I wanted to give off the impression that I had been in the industry a long time to show that I had knowledge and power to get people's homes sold. When I was lacking information, I had the motivation to learn everything and do right by my clients. I knew the industry had a lot of potential, but I'd have to put in a lot of elbow grease before I could reap any rewards. Having such an early success with my first client really inspired. It said there is money to be made here, I just had to work to make it happen. Every day, I spent hours learning the ins and outs of social media and how I could utilize it to boost my marketing efforts.

I incorporated everything I had learned about branding from my boutique business and started building out my logo, my brand, and my website. I created a business page on all the social media platforms, heavily focusing on Facebook to generate business. The results were as expected, the clients started to come in. I was producing enough closings to start bringing in a strong steady stream of income. We had never had money like this before. Finally, we were buying nice furniture for the house, affording good gifts for Christmas and birthdays for our daughters, and getting to a point where we could actually start a real savings account. When I finally had enough saved up to pay my aunt back, she refused to take the money, as was to be expected with her giving heart. So, I knew one day I'd be sure to give back to others in the way she gave so much to me.

I first started off with fairly low-end price points, then worked my way up. Eventually, I was getting a few high-end listings and worked my way into the luxury market. I spent hours every day growing my Facebook and Instagram following. I knew that if I spent productive time on those platforms, I could build my online sphere of influence and that would eventually translate into clients. I loved that there were no caps to how much money I could make and really scale into. For the first time in my life, I was getting paid good money. Heck, great money. The late nights, early mornings, and endless cups of caffeine were starting to really pay off. I made how much I wanted to make. I made how much I worked hard to achieve. I thought, wow, I have a real career making great money and despite the ever-present depression, that light at the end of the tunnel started to get brighter and bigger. I still wasn't where I wanted to be, I still wasn't making the kind of money I wanted to make, but I was getting even closer. I just had to grind away so the available opportunities before me would come to fruition.

When I wasn't out showing homes to a client, or meeting with potential sellers, I was looking for new ways to improve my business and marketing methods. Building a brand, if you're really passionate about it, isn't that hard. The hardest part is finding clients who will work with you. Clients, not only who will work with you, but can also make it to the closing table. Unlike any other business, where you generally get paid upfront, it can take months to see a paycheck in real estate. After you work with a client to land a contract, it can take 30 to 45 days to get to closing. If something happens along the way to blow the whole deal, which happened quite often, then you spent months working with someone and didn't make a single penny.

"Oh, Linda, that's awesome, you have 10 closings coming up next month?" always turned into, "Oh, Linda, that stinks that only one made it to the closing table."

When I'd think the next month was going to make me rich, I got lucky if I pulled a couple thousand out of it. Plus, with this business, you invest your *own* money into driving your clients around to show properties, or helping them prepare their house for the market, etc. It really puts a strain on entrepreneurs in this field to "make it." *Is* there a lot of money to be made? Yes, but you have to get to closing before you see anything out of it. If you aren't careful, you'll be out more money investing into your clients before you make a dime.

I not only focused on how to grow my business and brand, but I also had to figure out a way to streamline it, so I wasn't putting so much invested time on accounts that led nowhere except frustration. I can't tell you how many of my clients I cried alongside with, when only days before they were set to move into their dream home, something random came up in their credit history, and they were no longer approved to buy. As much as I loved real estate, I equally hated it.

It's a tough industry to navigate, your focus is not only consumed by building the brand that generates the business, but also figuring out how to automate it so you can scale, and about learning to target your marketing to find clients that have a better closing conversion. Like every agent that had come before me, if I wanted to become a true success in the industry, I had to figure out how to invest my time in people that could get to the final part of the transaction. Since real estate is a huge relationship-based business focused on referrals, and I was too anxiety ridden to cold call or door knock, I really had to figure out how to build relationships with people on social media in a way that gave them the trust to hire me. I don't know why, and I'm not sure if I'll ever figure it out, but I've had the luck of finding ease in drawing people's attention, and most importantly, getting people to trust me. Well, the trust part comes from being trustable, but was never a struggle to showcase how much I cared for my clients. I gave them the comfort of knowing that I would be a reliable source through the most expensive transaction in their lives.

Eventually, my hard work started getting noticed. Not only did I have a steady stream of clients, I was also getting recognized by other agents across the nation. They saw my branding, they saw my growth on social media, and people were reaching out wanting to know how I was doing all of this at such an early start to my career. To help other agents who were struggling just as I was, I started making videos and posting them on social media on how to grow their businesses on Facebook and Instagram. I was sharing everything I was doing in hopes that others would find the same success I did. My success was built on a foundation that was rare, in that most my marketing was being done for free. Sure, I advertised on Facebook ads, but 90% of my clients came through free marketing techniques I did on social media. I was asked to do video seminars, I was on podcasts, I was teaching a few classes here and there and growing in the real estate industry in a way that I hadn't expected.

Through that, I grew an amazing tribe of real estate agents. Although they weren't my market in the sense that they were the ones who brought in money like my buyers and sellers did, I still got to be a part of a community of other like-minded entrepreneurs that were focused on building a phenomenal life. I loved being a part of a community that also focused on other's success as much as their own. For the most part, everyone teamed up to help each other win in our industry. We had a few outliers that weren't team focused, but we worked with the people that were in it to win it for everyone.

The love and encouragement I was seeing from others motivated me to raise my bar in success and helped me focus on doing more meaningful things. We built a small community on Facebook that was focused on helping people find success on social media. At that time, I started having a lot of real estate agents approaching me, asking if I could make logos, websites, and other design work for them, that matched the quality of content I was putting out for myself, and they would pay me for my time. Although I was making great money with real estate, before I knew it, I had started a marketing and design company, specifically for real estate agents, so they could get a brand and presence that started generating real customers.

I had never gone to school for design, never went to learn anything about marketing, but by luck and hard work, I became a natural at it. The design company I had built to be a part time gig was now taking away my attention full time. The income was the same as I was making when I was selling real estate, but I was excited to be paid at the beginning of a project, instead of the end. Finally, I was getting paid upfront for the work I was doing, and I can't tell you, unless you've been an agent yourself, how much of a weight this lifts off your shoulders. No more spending weeks with a customer and crossing your fingers that you got paid. For design, I got paid, I did the work, and everyone was happy.

Through working one-on-one with agents, I noticed immediately how often the women were left to the backburner in our industry. Even though women made up 65% of real estate agents, it felt and looked like a male dominated business. I could see how this held a lot of women back from building a lucrative income. Being a woman myself, and seeing that struggle first hand, it motivated me to move away from the marketing community I had built for agents on Facebook, and instead focus on one specifically for women. And that's how the Ladies of Real Estate brand came to life. I didn't have much in mind for it, but just that I wanted to build a community of female real estate agents to help each other grow within our field. I put a lot of effort into the branding of Ladies of Real Estate to speak for the atmosphere I was trying to build for the group. That it was for empowerment, specifically for women, so they had equal opportunities to be in the spotlight and find success. It was a way to celebrate the ladies in our industry for their hard work. Surprisingly, it grew a lot faster than I expected, reaching over 5,000 members in a month and expanding rapidly. In one year, it reached 50,000 women – which was phenomenal!

Meanwhile, I was still working in graphic design for real estate agents. It was noticeable how many women struggled to pay for my services. Although I wanted things to be affordable and was pricing my material less than 75% of other designers in the industry, it was clear how many agents struggled to hire skilled graphic designers to bring their brand up to par to stand out in their market. That tugged at a cord in me. I was just like them when I first started off and most of them didn't have the know-how to build a beautiful brand presence on social media. They also had a hard time trying to figure out how to use that brand to then turn around and pick up buyers and sellers.

Here were thousands of female agents who were struggling, just like I was, and I wanted to help them. I knew my prices were out of most of their budgets, but I couldn't drop the prices I had for the work I was doing, or I'd be drowning in clients and not make enough to make ends meet. This was a unique dilemma to think through.

It was time to find a solution that helped me achieve my personal goals of success while helping others find their own success through hard times. Especially those who had no money to lean on for support, or a wonderful aunt that was able to pay their way into our industry. I was motivated to find an answer to help the women in my fast-growing community. I wanted to provide them opportunities to make money on the same level I did. It had to be affordable for them, but still paid enough to ensure my bills were taken care of. To be honest, I wanted growth and success of my own, so I had to figure out how to combine my success with theirs, hand in hand.

I started searching on other social media platforms for inspiration. Looked at ways to provide design at a rate that could be scaled, so that it could be produced for more agents at a lower cost. I looked at a variety of content on different platforms and industries and sought out a unique way to provide my services on a more efficient and affordable level. It was in that point in my life, living out of our small two-bedroom apartment with two little girls playing at my feet, that my stroke of genius finally hit. It was that moment that I came up with a business idea that not only would pull us out of all of our financial struggles, but it would also help us to get over $100,000 dollars of debt paid off. It was the amazing idea that put us in a half a million-dollar home, paid in cash, in one year after its conception. That's what it takes to be a success. Decades of hard work, suffering, searching and longing for something bigger and better, that something finally falls into your lap and makes you seem like an overnight success.

8.

GROWING A BUSINESS EMPIRE

After an extensive amount of research and seeing how other platforms worked, I came up with the plan to create a $20/month subscription, and I would share my design work on a template basis, that can be edited by the gals, to use in their own branding and marketing. On top of that, I provided coaching videos on exactly how I was generating business on social media. It was one tool for our community members on the Ladies of Real Estate group, to get a variety of productive tools to grow their business. Although I did believe the concept would succeed, since there wasn't anything like it out there, I did not expect it to explode in growth like it did. Within 3 months, I was making about $35,000 a month and growing. I invested a good chunk of money coming through from the subscription service and launched a variety of software and programs that complimented the real estate industry. Soon, I was making a little over $1 million in profit by the one-year mark. Just before year 2, we were well into a multi-million dollar business.

I was mind blown. Although I had always dreamed of reaching statistics like this, and knew I'd work endlessly until I did, it still felt surreal. The broken and abused girl who came out of a small town in the Middle East, a girl who statistics claimed would turn into a nobody based on my past and mental health, had finally grown into a woman with a multi-million dollar business by the age of 25. I had moved our family into a dream house, my husband and I had two beautiful daughters, and we were no longer financially struggling. For the first time in my life, I fell asleep in tears of happiness. I was finally giving my daughters the life I had always dreamed of giving them. Everything happened so fast and the success grew quickly. From years of experiencing a variety of industries, all stemming back from starting an online boutique while living in a crummy apartment, to now making millions from the hard work and knowledge I had built over time.

Through this journey, I learned there are three key elements to building a successful business. One, I had to learn what I was good at and passionate about. This took a bit of time to figure out, with experience in a variety of industries, before I realized design was even a world I could get into.

The second element is the people. When I first started the Ladies of Real Estate community, I was already doing graphic design and marketing, but never attributed it to my group of women. They were two separate entities. One was to empower female real estate agents and the other was to help all agents stand out through their branding. I focused on growing Ladies of Real Estate because I wanted to build a powerful network of real estate professionals that could motivate and encourage one another, but more importantly, build bonds with each other. Nothing is more encouraging than having a friend in the same industry that is pushing you to become the best version of yourself. Ladies of Real Estate was my community, it was my tribe. They were my backbone to growing myself on both a personal and professional level and I adored every one of them that engaged and helped motivate one another.

It was in the growth of LRE that I came up with our affordable subscription program, but I will tell you this, if it wasn't for that community of women, it would have been a lot more of a struggle to grow the company. I don't think I'd be making the kind of money I'm making now if it wasn't for the close relationships I built with them. They literally were the backbone of the business. So it was imperative that the community came first. I was already in real estate and I loved the industry. Through it, I got called to the back end of things in helping the agents instead of the buyers and sellers. I knew my tribe and what I was passionate about rested with them.

When I first got into real estate, everyone says the best conversion happens in your sphere of influence. That meant the people I knew on a regular basis. Friends on social media, friends and family in real life, etc. But I didn't have a sphere of influence when I started my real estate career in Nashville. Anyone I knew was already a real estate agent or related to one. So, I focused on building my sphere. I chose the online platform to grow it, because I was, and still am, an introvert.

Ladies of Real Estate became my sphere and they led to the success of my company. Without a sphere, I couldn't have succeeded. I also loved learning that I could build a sphere online, despite my anxious personality that didn't give me much room to feel comfortable in face-to-face settings. I didn't have to be this wild extroverted entrepreneur to build a successful company.

Another important note was knowing how to give value back to my ladies. It was about actually being there for the women and supporting them in their endeavors. I provided this support through free content. I made and gave away free designs all of the time, I made free coaching videos, and provided a large variety of tools to help them grow – without setting expectations to buy something from me. This gave them first hand experience with the quality of my content, then gave them the option to use my services if they enjoyed what they had for free. I gave and gave and gave, until the women wanted to give back by growing what the LRE community was. If I had just made the LRE Facebook group to spam everyone, it would have never grown as big as it is today, and I would have struggled convincing people the value of the membership.

The third element to making my business a success was coming up with a unique solution. This part took a lot of time and research to find a creative idea. I'd say it was the hardest part, but well worth the time and energy invested. I wasn't looking to build a business that already existed. I knew there were problems with what currently existed, my focus was to build something new that solved this problem. I learned what I needed to create by listening to the complaints of my tribe. The biggest complaint was that quality graphic design and coaching was too expensive. I had my problem. The solution was finding a way to provide everything they needed at an affordable rate, but in a way I could manage to do it alone.

This is where the research came in and helped me to come up with the idea of a template style subscription. It helped keep things affordable and made professional designs, related to our industry, available at their fingertips. I learned to listen to my audience and they were the ones who gave me the answer I needed to build a powerful business. I listened to their complaints and frustrations, and even implemented the issues I had a hard time with when I first started off.

In my search for this new business model, I didn't search for an answer in our industry. I already knew that what I was trying to build didn't exist, so I looked at what other industries had going on. My stroke of genius came from the beauty and fashion industry. I loved how the women focused on building their personal brands and creativity, and what they did to give back to their followers. Just like the real estate community, the beauty and fashion gurus had an industry that was inundated with competition, and I liked their methods to help themselves stand out. I applied what they were doing and put it to work with Ladies of Real Estate, because this massive female-focused community didn't exist in the real estate world. These days, there are a variety of companies that are mimicking our business model in real estate, but I felt a sense of pride for being the first to start this revolutionary trend for women.

It was that simple. However, simplicity can't be confused as easy, because that simplicity took years to figure out. Years of experience in other industries to learn where I was meant to be today. I wanted to be a millionaire, I knew one day it would happen, but knew it would require years of hard work to achieve it. Finally, I had hit the jackpot. Everything fell into place when I refused to give up. It all came down to those three elements: finding my passion, building my tribe, and coming up with a solution for an industry wide problem. I had no money, no influence, had a past of abuse and depression, and struggled talking to people because of my anxiety. In the end, none of that mattered. It was the willingness to succeed, and the work to make it happen, that brought me into the spotlight.

I think I succeeded, when a lot of people don't, because of my hunger, my motivation, and my addiction to wanting to work all the time. I spent the better half of my life being told by people that I was worthless, I wouldn't amount to anything, and I would always be a failure. Instead of listening and believing their emotional abuse, I decided I wanted to prove everyone wrong. Their words did affect me, it caused a massive amount of insecurities, but I wouldn't let that stop me from growing into a bigger and better person. Not only was I addicted to working hard, but also to proving the world wrong. *Who cares what they think*, I thought. This was my life and only mine to live, and I would create an outcome I saw fit, despite the mold everyone tried shoving me in.

Life is about being hungry and having realistic expectations. It was about investing time into growing and learning, and not allowing our personal insecurities and what others said, set a limitation on our growth. I spent as much time in educating myself as I did trying to grow the business. The more knowledge I gained, the more growth my business had. When I was broke, I knew I wasn't rich yet because I hadn't learned enough yet. The greatest part about growing up in my generation was all the online tools that provided education and training for free. YouTube, Google, Pinterest and Facebook came in handy when I had to learn how to find success without a penny to spend.

Now, anytime I create a business, I never focus on what I want. I focus on what my community, no matter what industry, needs from me. What solution can I figure out for a problem *they* have. A successful business has a story based around their customers, not about the owner. And I enjoyed learning that through growing LRE. Although it was an absolute passion to be a part of the real estate and graphic design industry, I knew it was finally time to transition into a career I had now spent the past 10 years thinking about – becoming an author.

Through the success of LRE, I was able to pursue my dream of becoming the author this bookworm has always wanted to be. By the age of 25, not only did I have a multi-million dollar business, I was finally getting to what I always wanted to do - write books. Growing up, reading was a cure for my soul. Now I wanted to pursue writing my own stories, both personal life experiences and fictional books. Call it destiny, or what you will, but I knew it was my calling. Not to write one book, but to become a successful author.

The Edge of Broken was going to be the first book I had ever intended to launch. I knew my personal life experience would be my first story, then after that, so many more would follow. Writing this book, and sharing my life story with you, would be just as much of a cleanse for my spirit as it would be motivational to women who may have gone through similar circumstances. It was written for those who needed a little proof that it doesn't matter what our circumstances and past were, we could and can always be the people we *want* to be. None of us have to become the people our pasts tried to define us as. We don't have to listen to those who tell us who we can or can't become. How long you were a victim to your life circumstances no long matters. If you have the will, the way, and the creativity, then you can accomplish anything. If the creativity is missing, then do enough research till something finally clicks. The lightbulb above our heads turn on for different people at different times in our lives. You just have to continue fighting through until it's your turn for it to light up.

Despite the success and wealth, one thing lingered heavily on my mind. Even with everything I now had, I still suffered with depression and severe anxiety. It didn't matter how much money I was making, how nice our home was, or how much I loved my family – the depression was still as strong as ever. Through my success, it would still be the hardest challenge I'd face on a daily basis.

9.

FACING MY DEMONS

For most people, depression comes in a wave that makes them feel lifeless and unmotivated to get up and get to work. Although I had my share of days like this, it didn't hinder my motivation to work on my business. However, it did impact me in a variety of other ways. The biggest was insecurity. I know everyone faces insecurity in themselves to some level, but mine became amplified by my depression. Have you ever looked in a mirror and cried because of how much you hated the way you looked? I have. Have you self-sabotaged relationships, even a marriage, because you made yourself think your partner thought horrible things about you, because that's how you felt about yourself? I certainly did. I hated myself. I hated the way I looked, I hated the way I felt weak, I hated how much of a victim I was to people in my past, and it filled my insides with anger and bleakness. I avoided the mirror as often as I could, further depressed by how much I had lost my body to my pregnancies. Every part of my body now needed Spanx to hold it off the ground and looking in a mirror naked was morbid enough to make me feel like I belonged in a freak show. Silly, of course, but when your insecurities are amplified by your depression, you think the worst about yourself, and I did.

I also believe that my depression held me back from further success. Most of the powerhouses in the real estate industry, who didn't have as large of a community as I did, had a bigger impact and outreach. Why? I had a crippling fear of putting myself on camera to do videos. In today's day and age, videos on social media are an essential part of massive growth. Even with this community of women I adored, and knew they adored and respected me back, I still had a hard time really putting myself out there. I laugh anytime anyone has ever complimented a video I did, or a podcast, because they didn't see the hours of cutting and editing I had to do to get rid of the heavy breathing from panic attacks. No one saw between sentence breaks all of the times I'd stop to comment on how stupid I was, or that no one would want to waste time listening to whatever I had to say.

I was horribly abusive to myself; ironically, even more so than the people I had grown up hating. I knew my biggest weaknesses, so I played on them every chance I got. It never mattered to me what people said about me, because I would sit around thinking something ten times worse. The years of emotional, physical, and sexual abuse left a lifetime's worth of personal abuse and insecurities. During parts of my life that I should have been the happiest, I turned into an uglier version of myself. When things went right in the world around me, they went wrong deep inside. I didn't know a good life, so I didn't trust the times I was going through a good time. When you spend most of your life in survival mode, you put your pain to the backburner, to collect overtime. So, when you finally get to a point in your life when you're thriving, and everything should be going right around you, all of the burdens you put aside now suddenly come back ten-fold in weight and pressure.

I was ecstatic about the success of my business and the financial stability its wealth brought for my family. However, that happiness didn't magically get rid of the decades of accumulated pain. Getting rich didn't make me happy. It bought me a nice house and brought comforts that lead to their own version of happiness, but deep inside, I was still the same broken little girl I had been my whole life. Money didn't fix that. Money wasn't a cure for depression or abuse. The most it could do was mask the pain for a short amount of time, but that pain would rear its ugly head around when you were least expecting it, because the money never got rid of it.

The biggest mistake I made during the growth of my business, and raising my daughters, was putting myself and my problems aside. I put myself in the dark, not paying any mind to how messed up I felt inside. In a period in my life when things should have been celebrated and full of joy, I was a broken woman. I fought constantly with my husband, never trusted anything he did – even when he wasn't doing a thing. I would get into huge fits of rage making claims that were only thought up in my mind, through my own insecurities and self-hatred. Then my anger at my husband would resonate towards my children. I'd be in a sour mood all day, angry and full of loathing at the whole world, and my daughters saw that in me. They'd avoid me, they wouldn't want to talk to me, and would always go to their dad - and that broke my heart.

I hated who I was. I couldn't stand the look of myself in a mirror and was feeling like a failure to my children. Online, the whole world saw me as a super hero for building this massive business empire and community.

However, at home, I was in a severely dark place and it was affecting my marriage and my children. My awful mood swings would ruin everyone's day. I wore my feelings on my sleeve, so when I was angry at the world, everyone around me could tell. The tension brewed deep inside of me, turning me into the ugliest version of myself I had ever seen. Rich or poor, this dark side of me lived and flourished, its thickness seemingly inescapable. I knew, if I didn't want my whole world to crumble at my feet, that I would have to address this monster that had grown inside of me. It didn't matter if I had money, if these emotions tore me away from the people I was trying to help. It didn't matter how beautiful my family was when I was pushing my husband and children away. Although I had spent my whole life refusing to be a victim to my past, I had lost all control of it when I chose to become this sad and angry person who despised everything and everyone in the world.

To be honest, I lived through daily phases where I hated people. I didn't understand life and it frustrated me. Knowing that I had survived and thrived through my abuse wasn't good enough for me, because I couldn't escape the horridness of the rest of the world. I couldn't stop thinking about the millions of others, right in this moment, who still suffered at the hands of evil and selfish people. My heart was a shredded mess thinking about the children who were still abused, most of them left to die alone in their pain and suffering. My heart was broken seeing all the people who ran to drugs and suicide, and I wondered how many of them had a story of abuse they chose to hold back, in fear of judgement. How many of them could have gotten help, but didn't, because they were so ashamed by what they had gone through?

The world, especially portrayed on social media, was filled with so many evil people that seemed to have an agenda to ruin as many people's lives as they could. It even affected my relationship with God, that I had thought my whole life was something unshakeable. I just wanted to know why. Why was there so much suffering? Why did the people that suffer the most were innocent children who had no hope of escaping their pain?

The more and more money I made, the more I hated it. The more it put in me in the spotlight, the more drama it brought in. I struggled with people already, now I seemed to face a new breed on these online platforms that spent days trying to make others miserable. I loved my tribe of supportive women, but their words seemed to always fall away when I was dealing with another "troll" that made attacks and attempts to defame my name and character. This did nothing for my hatred and anger towards the world, except worsen it. I slowly felt like I was drowning in this dark version of myself. I knew it was time to make a change after I saw how it impacted my relationship with my daughters. I couldn't let the cruelty of the world ruin the most beautiful connection I had ever made to any human being, and that connection was through them.

It was time to figure out a way for me to heal on a personal and emotional level. If I didn't, I'd lose everything in my life that I truly loved. Living in anger, no matter your circumstances, isn't living at all. You'll be quick to push away anything of substance in your life, and that's what I was doing. My anger, that stemmed from what terrible people did to me, was now being taken out on the people in my life that only wanted to love me and see me grow. The biggest realization, at this point in my life, was finally understanding that if I wanted to heal and become whole again, it would have to start from inside of me. This emptiness I spent a lifetime trying to fill could no longer be filled by other people or objects.

I spent my life chasing a romance, because I thought the right guy would fill the empty hole. When I still felt this emptiness inside, I then spent my life chasing money, because I thought building a successful business and finding some small level of fame would finally make me feel fulfilled. Although finding success did buy conveniences and security, it did nothing for my emotional well-being. I even thought having children would fill my emptiness, and although I found a love through them that I had never known possible, it still wasn't enough to fix my problems. I knew, if I wanted wholeness and peace, I'd have to find it within me. I could no longer search for it in other people or things.

Although I've always believed in God and leaned on Him to help me through my weakest moments in life, I was never a religious person. My connection to God has always been spiritual. I think, as humans, we're more in tune with nature and a spiritual side of the world then most of us come to terms with. Knowing and understanding the world on a more meaningful level gave me hope. It gave me encouragement to follow a path in life that was rooted in a powerful meaning. I never felt as fulfilled as I did when I was seeking the world in a way that was bigger than me, bigger than all of us. I find peace in knowing there is more to our story than what we see in the everyday situations. I find direction, and most importantly, I find self-healing.

My conversations with God are intimate and I feel comfortable talking about all the things that weigh on my heart. By saying my struggles out loud and thinking about them, and really coming to understanding and addressing them, I slowly started to build an understanding of my reactions and feelings. They say the best cure for an addict is to admit there is a problem, that's what I had to learn to do. In my anger and hatred, I justified how I felt because of my past. I justified my outbursts because I believed what I was thinking and feeling was right, with nothing breaking through my stubbornness to show me that I was actually in the wrong. You can't ever achieve anything in the right way when you approach it in anger. It was in these moments of peace, during meditation, that I'd address everything and understand the problems I had. In that understanding, I finally started to heal.

Meditation opened a side of myself I had shut away. It was the side of me that could process my past on an emotionally mature level. It was in the moments I'd close my eyes, and tune out the noise to relax, that I'd finally sense something different about myself. I started to change, I started to grow. My emotional and mental well-being shifted significantly. It was in those moments I'd have conversations with myself about what I knew was right in the world, right with me, even. I no longer had to listen to how others viewed me, because it meant more in the end how I viewed myself. I learned to become my own friend, my own rock, and my own source of security. I had to stop running away from myself and the broken parts that were left unhealed. This was my body, this was my shell, and if I wanted to find happiness, I had to learn how to mend her.

I always meditated outside, it felt right to be outdoors. I did it occasionally inside, but there was a different atmosphere to the experience when I was in nature. I turned off all my electronics, checked out for 15 to 30 minutes, and listened. Listened to the voice that whispers to all of us our inner wisdom. I'd tune into everything around me that mattered. The birds sung, the calming breeze caressed my cheek, the deer grazed in our backyard, and my daughter's laughter in their rooms always reminded me how simple and peaceful life could be if we chose to live in those quieter moments.

I found so much strength and peace in myself. When you shut the world out and listen to your inner being, you'd be surprised by the amount of wisdom that you can pull. I don't think that wisdom comes directly from within us, but a larger part of who we are in a spiritual sense. I grew up in a world full of strict religious-based families, from Christian to Muslim, and anything else in between, and I just never found myself at home in religion. However, when I took the time to find myself on a spiritual ground and reached out to God with the understanding that if I allowed him to help me cleanse my soul of all the anger and pain, he'd come in and do it.

I'd envision this burning white light that would come through the top of my head and slowly make its way out through my toes, grabbing and pushing out any form of darkness it came across along the way. I began to feel cleansed. I learned to breathe out my worst thoughts. Through these moments, that I gave back to myself to really learn who I was and what made me happy, I found peace. I understood, that through the fires of my childhood now stood a woman who endured and went on to build something the world said she couldn't, and that was something to be proud of.

I forced myself to look at things in new perspectives. When someone lashed out, instead of reacting in an equally negative tone, I took the time to force myself to understand that their pain and the way they address it is different than my own. Although I may not internally understand it, it didn't give me the right to hate them for it. This process would be one that would take a lifetime to master, but I started to feel the changes. I started to find a patience I never knew I had, I started to find a peace I never thought could exist.

Although my heart still hurt from the continuous suffering happening around the world, sitting around in anger at the world helped no one. In fact, it contributed to all of the bad things. Anytime I sat around loathing people and how cruel our lives were, I realized I was turning into the spiteful people I claimed to hate. It started to dawn on me that I wasn't better than the people I didn't like. I'd never be this perfect angelic person that was always full of happiness and sunshine, it just wasn't my identity, but I could learn to let go of all the anger that ran through my veins. So, I did.

This whole time in my life, I refused to let the people who hurt me, win. To ensure they didn't, I focused on building materialistic successes to show off the person I had become. But in fact, they were still winning all along. Because it didn't matter how many things I had, or how much money I had made, or how big my house was, if I was a disaster internally. For every word I spoke in anger, the people who hurt me won. For every insecurity that made me cry or mope in depression, the people who had hurt me had won. For every time my daughters watched me screaming and crying at my husband for something I blamed him for doing, that he was innocent of, the people who had hurt me had won.

If I wanted to really prove to the world that I wouldn't be a victim to my past, it wasn't the outside of my life that needed to change, it was the inside that needed to heal. Even when you push the worst sides of yourself to the back of your mind, where you aren't consciously thinking of it on a daily basis, it is still there molding you into becoming someone you'll despise. You have to address your worst traits. You have to address your worst fears. You have to pull into the light the things that hurt you the most. There is no healing in the darkness. That wound will never heal, because hidden away on your back, it festers as an infection that poisons your heart and mind. You have to open up your wounds, so you can clean them, and finally give them the opportunity to heal. Nothing gave me the opportunity to address these things like going outside, shutting off my electronics, to meditate and address everything that was wrong with me. That I thought was wrong with me.

I was tired of hating the world. I was tired of seeing it in such fogged over glasses that only showed the bleakness and darkness of it. I was ready to clean my sight and see the world for what it truly was. The world was full of beautiful people. A lot of beautiful people that had gone through their own version of pain. So many of them in the same boat as me, living in their anger and hatred of the world, that they don't give anybody a chance in fear that they'll get hurt again. I believe that's why the world continues in its cycle of hatred and depression. That's why the news is filled with horrific crimes and terrible events. All of us have a pain in one form or another and we choose to hide away from that pain, blaming the whole world for our scars, instead of the few people who were the only ones that hurt us.

That's why we are drawn to the negative side of things. That's why when horrific incidents happen, news channel views go up, because we love to be right. We love to say, "See, this world *is* an awful place, I hate people and never want to be around anyone." We live in this putrid atmosphere, that although we think is outside of us, we contribute to daily. I was always fascinated by the few souls I met through my life that seemed to always be happy. Even when life was in shambles for them, they'd have this genuine smile and light beaming from within them. Have you ever met a person like that? If you have, you'll never forget them. Even if you forget their name, their face will always linger in your mind when you think of what happiness is.

I always thought, why can't I be like them? Why am I so full of darkness? Even people who have gone through a great deal of loss can learn to be happy, why can't I? But I could. I just never gave myself the opportunity to. I never forgave myself for feeling like a weak victim to the people who hurt me. I never forgave myself for feeling ugly after years of hearing it from others. I never forgave myself for the weak moments I was forced to do horrific things to my sexual abusers. I never forgave myself for showing weakness every time I cried in front of someone who had hurt me. But you can't heal, and you can't move on, without forgiveness. We're told that our whole lives to forgive and move on, and yet, no one talks about forgiving ourselves? Even as victims to tragic circumstances, we subconsciously blame ourselves for the things that went wrong. What if I wasn't there that day. What if I had gone with option A instead of option B. What if I had just fought back? What if, what if, what if.

Relationship coaches tell us that we can't love someone else without loving ourselves first, but that doesn't just apply to finding a soul mate. That applies to everything in life. You can't find friends if you can't be your own friend. You can't be nice to others if you aren't being nice to yourself. You can't expect the world to rid itself of anger if you're consumed by anger every day. You can't expect the world to rid itself of its sadness, if you spend your days moping around in depression. You can't expect the world to get off their electronics and enjoy people as they are, if you hide every time someone comes and knocks on the door. Through all of these quiet moments of self-reflection, I learned so much. In that knowledge, came maturity. In that maturity, came self-worth. In that self-worth came healing.

Who was I to expect something of others, when I was failing to be the person I expected others to be. It wasn't others hurting me anymore. It wasn't the world I hated. It was me. I hated myself, I was hurting myself. I only saw through anger and lived in its shadow, then yelled at anyone who was doing the same thing, in a slightly different output. I was such a hypocrite. To expect the world to be a better place without forcing myself to become a better person to start with.

During these moments of time I gave back to myself, to meditate and expose everything I saw wrong in the world, I realized it was everything I was seeing wrong in me. Figuring out what was wrong with me wouldn't fix it overnight. I knew, if I truly wanted to live a life of joy, that I had to expect to be in this change for the long haul. If I wanted to be a great mother to my children, a great wife to my husband, a great neighbor, friend, or relative – I needed to focus every day on becoming a better version of who I was the day before.

Did coming to this realization make the anger disappear instantly? Absolutely not. Even today, I feel it lingering; but, I know I'm healing and that it's a process to get through. Just like an infected wound, it won't heal overnight. This pain was a chronic wound from a lifetime of suffering, and it was going to take time for it to heal. Even when it heals, it'll still have the scar to remind us of who we once were. It's a process, but we have to be willing to take that process through to the long haul. It's necessary in order to find a better version of ourselves and a better version of our world. This applies to everybody. Whether you're religious or not. Whether you're spiritual or not. You have to first become the person you expect others to be. You want others to stop being judgmental? You have to stop judging. You want others to be happy, and not angry all of the time? You have to learn to be happy and get rid of your anger. You want people to stop being lazy? Well, what part of your life are you slacking on? Change begins with us and within us. My pain started in the hands of other people, but I had the choice to change how I felt from here on out.

If you believe this is the only life we're given, then why do we choose to constantly live in such an ugly version of ourselves? Why do we put so much energy into other things that have no substance, instead of investing into our own mental clarity and well-being? We huff and say, "Who has time for that?" Yet, you waste so much time on social media. We claim to others, "There isn't a thing wrong with me." But you know there is, because you go to bed most nights angry or in tears.

We have to accept that we're all a broken mess. From one circumstance in our life to another, we've been wounded. When that wound wasn't addressed immediately, it infected us and made us a poisoned version of ourselves. That poisoned version now poisons the rest of the world. I know with billions of people in the world, that it can be hard to think that we could change this world for something better than what it seems to be. But even with such large numbers, no one will change anything in this world until they learn to change themselves. If half of the world looked at themselves and said enough is enough and chose to no longer be vile or angry or depressed, then the whole world wouldn't have to change for the whole world to change. If we changed ourselves, instead of trying to change others, the results would be more drastic. Is this idealistic thinking? Will the whole world actually change? Maybe, maybe not. But we won't know that until you start to change yourself. I often thought, how could I expect the hate in the world to disappear if I continued to hate the world?

This was a powerful revelation. It forced me to see the world in a new perspective. Did horrific things happen to me in my life? Yes. Does it mean the whole world is a horrific place to be a part of? No. It may feel like it, if you're living through your pain now, in whatever version it's being presented to you. However, no matter how horrific our situations can be on an individual level, it is not a definition of the world and its people as a whole. We just see it in that filter because we put that filter over our own eyes based on our personal feelings. If I thought about it, the people who were kind to me in my life were 100 to 1 in comparison to the people who took part in trying to destroy my life. Yet, I chose, like most people, to focus only on the negative view of the world. I put hundreds of people, who had nothing but kind words to share, off to the side, so I can mope over the few people who said and did hurtful things. Now, how does that make sense?

I was determined to make a change in myself and I would. I'd stop making the ugly side of life a priority, they were nothing more than a speed bump to get over. Some of those bumps are so big that they leave us unable to move for a while, but those bumps in our lives don't define the world as a vile place that hates us. The world didn't hate me, I just thought it did, because I chose to hate it.

Adding a new filter to the way I viewed life finally began the healing process and I felt like a different person. Perspective changes everything. I realized that the weakest moments in my life were the days I learned how to be the strongest version of myself. For every person that said I was stupid, there were many more to uplift and encourage me for how wise I was. Life is always about how you choose to perceive it. If you choose to see it in a dark and dirty filter, it'll always appear that way. If you choose to wipe the dirt off your eyes, and see the dark corners and shadows brighten up, then life will seem brighter as a whole. Easy to write, easy to think, but not always easy to live by on a day to day basis. But that's okay. It's understanding it that gets you on the path to healing. It gets you on the path for becoming a better version of yourself. Understand the issues within yourself and you'll be surprised by how much you understand the issues in the world.

We all may lead different lives, but it's wonderfully bizarre how similar we all are. I'm still fascinated by all of the new people I meet, and once we start sharing our stories in an intimate way, how much we think and feel alike. These people I would have turned away from and hated in my past, were just like me. They had been hurt, their trust in people shredded and now, they just wanted one person to show them the world could be a better place than the lonely solitude they lived in. For every anger they had, it was only a self-defense mechanism for the pain they had endured. Their fear of getting hurt led to isolation. Their isolation led to anger. These weren't people who *wanted* to be spiteful, they just didn't know how to be any other way, because of what they went through. After focusing on personal healing and personal growth, I knew I needed to get out there and do what I feared doing most, talking to people, face-to-face. It wasn't until I had intimate conversations with strangers, that I started to finally fill this empty void.

I realized, healing began with me, but it ended with the rest of the world. I couldn't heal, then stop there. I had to finally confront the world I had despised my whole life. It was time to see the people in a colorful way, instead of the dark picture I had painted them as. Was I afraid of being betrayed and hurt, again? Of course, but I realized it was human nature to make mistakes. I had to learn to navigate other people's bad decisions by learning not to take it personal. It was just a part of their lives they had to work through on their own. I wouldn't let that hold me back from experiencing the power of people. It was time to open up to a world I had spent my whole life shutting out.

10.

POWER IN PEOPLE

How do you see the world in a new pair of eyes? By engaging in it and seeing it through the eyes of others. In my worst moments, I not only hated the world, I hated people individually. I saw everyone's flaws. I put everyone into the same shadows I put my abusers in. I refused to make eye contact with anyone, to prevent people from talking to me. I pushed people away from trying to be my friend because I was sure they were after something more. I wasn't being mean, but I was reserved. I was nice when I had to be but closed myself up before anyone could take advantage of that kindness.

The only exception to that was children. I opened my heart to them without hesitation. I saw their innocence, and their weakness because of that innocence, as I saw in myself when I was a child. To the rest of the world, I turned myself to ice; but to kids, I saw myself as their protector. I saw vulnerabilities in them that most people were blind to. Aside from them, other people were the enemies. I hid away from neighbors who tried visiting and didn't ever bother engaging with anyone trying to sell me a religion or product. I hid from everyone. As I watched the mailman drop off a box at my door and ring the doorbell, I wouldn't open it till he drove away. I laugh at my reactions, thinking about them now, but that was engrained in my identity. I chose to believe that everyone had an agenda and instead of allowing them to prove otherwise, I lived in those thoughts and justified my feelings by convincing myself I was right.

I had lost all sensibility in that time in my life. I'm sure God shook his head in frustration with me one too many times. If I was to make a comparison, I was easily worse than Wednesday from the Addams Family. It was who I had become. It was who I had *allowed* myself to become. But it was time to stop hiding.

Moving forward, I made a better effort to spend more time with people. I spent more time with family members I had ignored for months. I spent time with neighbors and built bonds with them and their families. Getting to talk to and enjoy the company of these wonderful people made me feel so silly for ever ignoring them in the past. Although I still remained a little reserved in the people I chose to give my time to, I opened myself up in ways that I'd never done before. I shared with people my personal story, my journey, and my pain. I was shocked to see how well people took my past, and how encouraging they were for my perseverance. But nothing was as eye-opening as hearing the similar journeys others had had. It was unbelievable how many others had endured abuse, especially childhood sexual abuse.

I never thought I was the only victim to sexual abuse, but childhood abuse feels like an isolated pain. Most abuse victims don't talk about what they've gone through, it's almost like taboo to mention you've been beaten, molested, or raped. There is a stigma around it that shames victims and forces them to silence. The culture around it is a big part of why it's still so prevalent today. And it *is* prevalent, in massive numbers. It happens to both men and women. When you open up and have conversations with people about it, you'll see there are millions who have endured the same pain. This was baffling. The American culture condemns child abuse, especially incest, and yet it happens behind the closed doors of millions of homes. We condemn other countries for their disgusting and perverse treatment of women and children, and yet it happens in our own backyards just as significantly. The difference? They boast about it in other countries, we just sweep our abuse under the rug and pretend it doesn't exist.

All this time I had spent shutting out the whole world, others suffered the same fate I had. Not only did I betray myself by shutting out other people, I betrayed all victims of abuse. By staying hidden in my anger and pain, I contributed to the culture that avoids talking about it. By refusing to talk to other people about the abuse that goes on in the world, I had a small hand in letting it continue to happen to other innocent victims. I couldn't hide away, ashamed of what had happened to me, if I wanted to prevent it from happening to other innocent children. I was so wrong for hating people. Their hearts bled the same tears mine did, and all of them just needed someone who could relate with, someone who could understand their pain.

It was an awe-inspiring realization. If we took the time to know each other, listen to each other, and open up to one another without fear, we could share so much love and healing with one another. We could turn the darkest sides of ourselves into people who knew how to love again. Learned how to be happy again. If I wanted the world to change, I had to be a part of that change. I had to open myself to conversations I was too afraid of having before.

The wisdom that grows from those conversations can give us all the power to make a difference.

Will there be people who turn your story around and use it as a tool to hurt you? Sure, there may be a couple. But that will only be a negative impact on you if you choose to let it be a negative impact. It's perspective. Sharing your journey about your own pain doesn't mean there is something wrong with you. If someone sees a negative in that and tries to use it against you, the only problem lies with them. Knowing that should give you strength. No one has the power to affect you in any way unless you *choose* to give them that power. And why would you let someone's opinion of you hold you back, when you've already endured and conquered through so much? Who cares if someone said ugly things about me, I just survived years of abuse and turned my life around to make it something amazing. I have a beautiful life, a beautiful family, a successful business. Who cares if one or two people in the world want to say something ugly about that? That's not a "you" problem, that's a "them" problem. You have to understand that they must have gone through something awful, and this is their way of reacting to the world because of their own pain. It has nothing to do with you. You're an absolutely beautiful soul who has endured so much and lived to fight on. Don't let the opinions from other broken people convince you otherwise.

I know this can be hard to accept, but it takes time to re-adjust your mindset to one that motivates you, instead of holds you back. I remember when I first started my motivational Facebook page, I always talked about depression and the pain I had gone through and how absolutely crippling it was. Well, one day I found someone sharing my page, making statements that I was mentally ill because I talked about my depression. They commented that I was sick and full of problems. I was hurt. I even unpublished my page. I didn't think twice about the 50+ comments from other women who were making statements about their own personal journey with depression. I ignored the women who were applauding me for being open, because it gave them the courage to talk about their problems. I let this one angry person, hiding behind a fake account, scare me away from making a connection with others.

A couple of days later, I thought to myself, what in the heck is wrong with you? Look at all these women who have been in similar shoes and are afraid to speak up because of bullies, and I'm cowering away because of one. I was doing a disservice to the people who needed a voice by letting this one spiteful person get to me. I re-published my page and swore I'd never make a decision based on the opinion of someone else. They were far and few between. What benefit did I have to other victims, or even myself, if I continued to hide away from the world because it has some darkness in it? I already knew it could sometimes be dark, but I made myself the promise to stop letting that make an impact on my decisions. No more hiding, Linda. No more being scared, angry, or sad. No more being intimidated by the few people in the world that *tried* to hurt me. No one had power unless I gave them power. From now on, the only people I gave power to were those who loved and supported me.

I could have listened to that ugly person online and hide away forever. But then, I wouldn't be here, in your hands, connecting with you. I made the choice to put myself out there. I chose to listen to the other women, whose cries could be heard in their voices, and connect with them. I could encourage them to live and fight on; but most importantly, remind them that they are loved. Did I think catty things every time someone said something ugly to me? I sure did. But when I did, I learned to re-focus and stop giving priority to things that added no value to my life.

The negatives were the things in life I took notice of, then needed to forget about in seconds. I had to force myself to start prioritizing the positive things in my life. I had to hold on to kindness, instead of focusing my energy on that one ugly thing that happened that one time that I had no control over. We all do that. If you posted a picture of yourself online and 100 people commented on how beautiful you were, but one person said your hair cut doesn't look good on you - instead of focusing on what those 100 people said, you'd obsess over that one negative comment. Most people will look in the mirror, make a comment about what an idiot that person is, and claim they look great. Which is where those thoughts should stop, but they don't. Because subconsciously you start thinking that maybe they were right, maybe your hair cut does kind of look funny. And before you know it, you're putting in extensions or going to the hairstylist for a new look.

I know most of us do that, and I'm not alone in it, because of the conversations I'd have with others about it. We are drawn to the negative EXACTLY like a moth to a flame. We all know what the heck happens to that moth when it reaches the flame, yet we live by the same measure. We are drawn to everything wrong with the world, and with ourselves, until we burn up into ashes because of it.

There is so much power in people. But that power is the power you give them. This gave me the knowledge to approach others in the right way. Instead of hating everyone and seeing the majority of people as evil and out to get me, I focused on the majority of people who were kind-hearted and fighting their own struggles. On the rare occasion I faced someone being cruel, I deleted them and blocked them from my life. The only energy I gave them was a small prayer that they were able to find healing in their anger. No more power to them, now the power laid with the right people.

The more people I spent time around, the more I realized how lonely my life had been. How mundane and lacking joy it was till now. That hole, that I couldn't fill my whole life, was finally starting to close. All because of self-healing, meditation, and through getting to know more people on a personal level. From taking the time to understand them, know them, and love them for who they were - flaws and all.

I began to feel an incredible transformation within myself. This angry lonely girl was starting to break through her shell, allow people into her life to tell their stories, and build wonderfully personal relationships. The world took on a whole new light and I now knew what I hungered for. A connection with people, all over the world. I chased silly romances, and although I found my wonderful husband, it didn't fulfill me. I chased money and fame, hoping the sense of accomplishment would take care of it, but none of that worked. My healing came through connection, it came through motivating and encouraging others, and it came through making an impact in people's lives that encouraged them to go out and make an impact for others.

I knew it was time. Time to write my story, time to take all I've invested into the wrong things and turn them around to invest into the right things. It didn't matter to me how rich I became. It didn't matter to me how "famous" I was. I found fame and money, and it did nothing for me. I wanted more intimate connections with people around the world. People with beautiful cultures, amazing stories, and their unbelievable strength to heal and persevere. This would be my fulfillment. This would be my journey, this would be the thing that filled my heart and soul.

I set out to see God's people and see His world. It was time to shut off the electronics and stop investing so much time into online platforms that regurgitated all the negativity. It was time to unplug, recharge, and revisit the life that we were meant to live in community. The power was in the people. The power was in our beautiful world. I just had to stop hiding from it and finally see it in person.

11.

BECOMING WHOLE AGAIN

My journey had begun. The first trip I took was to the country I had wanted to visit my whole life, Scotland. Not sure why, but for as long as I could remember, visiting Scotland would not only become a dream come true, it would be a lifetime achievement. It was the country I had envisioned full of magic and endless possibilities, and I knew that if I could make it there, I could make anything happen. I finally made that dream come true and had the pleasure of getting to experience it with my family. We made wonderful connections with the locals and enjoyed their beautiful culture. This was one of many trips around the world that were to come. Scotland was the starting point to knowing I could achieve all of my goals, everywhere else we went would have a focus on people.

I was hooked on seeing the world. I would seek its treasures, meet its wonderful people, and soak in all of its beauty. Even in the struggles and darkness I'd stumble across, I knew I'd focus on only seeing the light within it. This was to be my new life, my calling. To journey to every corner of the world and to share my experiences through my books. I used to drown myself in books, because it seemed that that was the only place I could find happiness. Now that I've found happiness in the real world, I knew I wanted to write books that inspired and encouraged others, like they did for me when I lived through the pain. I wanted to make an impact through stories and tales that motivated and inspired. I want the words I write to influence others to pursue their dreams and learn how to become the best versions of themselves. Our future doesn't have to be ruined because of a bad past or upbringing. It's the belief in ourselves, and the willingness to work tirelessly to achieve our dreams, that should define us. I've accomplished a lot of things in my life, but I still have a long way to go before I become the person I want to be. I'm sure you do too, but you have to start today, before tomorrow is too late.

I hope my journey through abuse and loss connects with you through your own journey. I hope my path to finding success and growing a beautiful family inspires you. I also hope my story of finding happiness motivates you to chase after what makes you happy and fulfilled. The slightest influence in helping you seek the best version of yourself helps me get a step closer towards my personal fulfillment of changing the world, in what small way I can. Find your courage, love yourself, and know there is opportunity present in every difficult part of your life. No matter where your story begins, it can end how you want it to.

No more living in anger. No more living in fear and pain. No more hiding away from a world that is full of more beauty and light than bad things. No more focusing on an awful past, it's time to focus on your future. You've come a long way, and although you still may have a lot further to go, find strength in how much you've endured to get to where you are today.

I'm not going to tell you not to chase money; I did, and it bought conveniences. I'm not going to tell you not to chase romances; I did, and I found my husband through it. But understand, materialistic things will never provide a solution to resolving our worst traits. That comes from forgiving yourself and forgiving the rest of the world. It comes from self-healing, then sharing what you've learned to help others heal. It's getting out and seeing the world, as much and as often as you can, and learning to find more friendship and love in people. It's prioritizing your family and helping them to see a better side of you, so they can learn to find a better side of themselves. It's about making impacts, no matter how big or small, that are meaningful.

Don't get consumed by the hatred of this world. Don't be defined by the pain in your heart. On your weakest days, on the days when you hurt the most, find strength inside of you and mold it. Mold it to become better, to expect better, and to achieve better. Pain is a teacher and it shows all of us who we truly are on our worst days. You are not defined by your worst circumstances, but by how you choose to move on from them.

Find inspiration in what makes you happy, then pursue it with all of your energy. What makes me fulfilled won't necessarily be your fulfillment, but seek it in people and powerful relationships, instead of materialistic things. Man-made items are meant for convenience, not happiness. That fancy car or the brand-new house may seem like it leads to happiness, but it's temporary. If you're broken inside, no car or house will fulfill that. Meditate. Talk to yourself. Know yourself. Address the part of you that is angry, sad, or broken. Forgive that side of you, understand it, and learn how you can then start to heal from it. Find wisdom within you. It *is* within you. You just have to give yourself a chance.

And remember, finding love in the world starts by finding love in yourself. Finding friends in the world is becoming a friend to yourself. Seeing the light in the world, begins by chasing out the darkness within yourself. We have a lot of a lot work left to do, but we've begun our journey with our connection to each other. This is my story. What's yours?

ACKNOWLEDGEMENTS

First and foremost, I have to thank you, my Ladies of Real Estate tribe. A few years ago, I threw together a Facebook group in hopes of making it a phenomenal community for women in the real estate industry. Not only did you help me grow Ladies of Real Estate into the empire it is today, I found a community of supportive women. Women who were dedicated to giving back to each other in hopes of helping one another succeed. If it wasn't for your support, through all of my adventures, I wouldn't be where I am today. When I nervously and awkwardly made videos and podcasts, you were there to listen. When I shared my frustrations about what was lacking in the real estate industry, you were there to help me build a solution for all of us. Although I'm leaving that chapter of my life behind to pursue my dreams of becoming an author, I'm never leaving you behind. Not only did you give me the foundation for success with our marketing company, you have also given me the foundation for success for my books. Your pre-orders, encouragement, and sharing on social media have made this woman's dreams come to fruition. Through all of our bumps and bruises, I've learned so much from you amazing women. Thank you for supporting me, thank you for empowering me, and thank you for seeing the worth to invest in the things I create. I would probably still be stuck in my past emotions if it weren't for your support in getting me to where I am today.

I also want to acknowledge my husband and two beautiful daughters who have experienced this wild journey with me from the beginning. I'm so blessed to live through all of my dreams with you three by my side. I wouldn't have it any other way. Through the endless caffeine, mood swings, sleepless nights, and snappy days – you were there to encourage me with my dreams of becoming an author. I wouldn't be complete without you in my life.

A big thank you for my parents, Cameron's parents, siblings, and dear friends who have encouraged and supported me in this new adventure. You helped mold me into finding the courage to get my story into the hands of the world.

ABOUT THE AUTHOR

Linda Ward is an author, podcast personality, in-demand speaker, and founder of Ladies of Real Estate and Quill Press. LRE is a powerful online community supporting the success of female real estate agents, and Quill Press is a supportive community for female authors and readers. Linda uses the trials of her past to encourage women to find self-healing through their pain and struggles. She also uses her personal success as a way to motivate millions of women around the world to fight for their own dreams.

Linda resides with her husband and two children in Nashville, Tennessee.

For business inquiries, speaking gigs, or book-signing events, please contact us at hello@sincerelylinda.com or visit us at www.SincerelyLinda.com

I'd Love Your Support!

If you enjoyed this book, I would love your support by sharing it on your Facebook or Instagram page. It's my dream to start more conversations about the struggles women and children face in our world, and I have hope to encourage others to find their own success despite the circumstances of their past.

If you've faced your own personal trials, no matter what they are, please talk to someone about them. There is nothing more healing than having conversations with people who understand. If you feel alone, please connect with us on Facebook or through our website. We'd love to be there for you!

www.Facebook.com/SincerelyLindaOfficial
www.SincerelyLinda.com

Made in the USA
Middletown, DE
10 September 2018